Paris Monographs in American Archaeology 41

Sex, Metaphor, and Ideology in Moche Pottery of Ancient Peru

Andrew Turner

BAR International Series 2739
2015

Published in 2016 by
BAR Publishing, Oxford

BAR International Series 2739

Paris Monographs in American Archaeology 41
Editor: Eric Taladoire

Sex, Metaphor, and Ideology in Moche Pottery of Ancient Peru

ISBN 978 1 4073 1398 6

BAR Publishing is the trading name of British Archaeological Reports (Oxford) Ltd.
British Archaeological Reports was first incorporated in 1974 to publish the BAR
Series, International and British. In 1992 Hadrian Books Ltd became part of the BAR
group. This volume was originally published by Archaeopress in conjunction with
British Archaeological Reports (Oxford) Ltd / Hadrian Books Ltd, the Series principal
publisher, in 2015. This present volume is published by BAR Publishing, 2016.

Printed in England

BAR
PUBLISHING

BAR titles are available from:

BAR Publishing
122 Banbury Rd, Oxford, OX2 7BP, UK
EMAIL   info@barpublishing.com
PHONE   +44 (0)1865 310431
FAX   +44 (0)1865 316916
www.barpublishing.com

Acknowledgements

There are several people who deserve special thanks for providing invaluable assistance throughout the course of research and preparation of this manuscript. First, I would like to thank David Davison, Eric Taladoire, and an anonymous reviewer at BAR for their assistance in preparing this manuscript for publication and their helpful comments.

I am grateful to Stella Nair and Jason Weems, my thesis Co-Chairs, for the vast amount of time they invested into improving the quality of my work, and for continuously challenging me to approach the material in greater depth. Karl Taube and Jeanette Kohl offered thoughtful critiques and suggestions, and the quality of the finished product is greatly improved thanks to their help and support. Jeffrey Quilter graciously met and corresponded with me and offered his thoughts on this manuscript. I wish to express my profound gratitude to for his willingness to share his time and expertise, and his kind-natured enthusiasm for assisting young scholars.

I am indebted to Ulla Holmquist, Isabel Collazos T., and Andrés Álvarez Calderón of the Museo Larco. This project would not have been possible without their assistance and generosity in sharing their time, resources, and insights. Travel to Peru was possible through generous support from the Richard G. Carrott Memorial Fund through the University of California, Riverside, Department of History of Art.

Alejandra Martínez-Berdeja, Eric Heller, and German Loffler deserve my sincere thanks for giving advice, enthusiasm, and helpful suggestions at every stage of this process. I thank Raúl A. Martínez Calderas for kindly providing a Spanish translation of the abstract, and Eric Heller for his assistance in preparing some of the figures. Finally, I wish to express my gratitude to my family, George and Linda Turner, Britton, Ami, Alek, and Luka Purser, and Edith Wright, for their love and support.

Resumen

Escenas representando coito aparecen frecuentemente en el arte de la antigua cultura Moche de la costa norte de Perú (AD 200 a 900); no obstante, los significados detrás de tales imágenes permanecen escasamente entendidos. Un obstáculo potencial a la interpretación de las imágenes sexuales es una tendencia entre investigadores a abordar las imágenes Moche como representativas en lugar de con contenido simbólico o metafórico. Este estudio se enfoca en una serie de bajo relieves y escenas pictóricas de la alfarería Moche que describen una deidad con colmillos aludida como Cara Arrugada (también llamada Aipaec), copulando con una mujer. Las escenas son interpretadas como porciones de una narrativa mitológica más amplia, y tales escenas representan a Cara Arrugada ocupado en una cópula, probablemente originarias del sitio sureño de Moche, Huacas de Moche (Huaca de la Luna y Huaca del Sol). Los métodos de producción de las escenas mitológicas en alfarería hecha en molde de los centros huaca sugieren esfuerzos a favor de una clase sacerdotal o gobernante para controlar el contenido de tales mitos e incrementar su influencia a través de su distribución.

Análisis de las escenas implicando a Cara Arrugada sugieren que él es una deidad representando la montaña y que la mujer con quien él tiene un encuentro sexual es de la costa. Las escenas narrativas incorporan metáforas visuales que combinan montaña, ríos, *chicha*, guano y semen, vinculando procesos ambientales, tales como el ciclo del agua de las montañas a la costa, a la sexualidad humana y la reproducción. Las montañas fueron asociadas con la masculinidad y los valles ribereños que son fertilizados por el agua de las montañas y que rinden las cosechas son femeninos. De este modo, la reproducción humana es un evento microscópico que hace eco de fenómenos ecológicos a gran escala que son necesarios para la sobrevivencia en la costa árida.

Las escenas de copulación de Cara Arrugada pueden representar el origen mítico de la gente costeña, presentando a Cara Arrugada como un ancestro capital. Las imágenes que asocian a Cara Arrugada con los árboles que producen frutos sugieren que el papel de Cara Arrugada era semejante a las concepciones quechua de ancestros venerados. Las escenas que describen un encuentro sexual mítico entre Cara Arrugada y una mujer de la costa transmiten temas de ascendencia, regeneración y fertilidad agrícola, y presentan un modelo funcional para las labores de un cosmos vital dentro del cual la reproducción humana es una parte integral. Promoviendo a Cara Arrugada como un progenitor, Huacas de Moche pudo haber intentado reemplazar genealogías locales y reclamar acceso privilegiado a las fuerzas que hacen posible la vida en la costa. El claramente legible estilo visual Moche podría haber dado un sentido de veracidad a las escenas descritas, aún los significados simbólicos más allá de las apariencias inmediatas podrían ser patentes para los practicantes de los sistemas de creencias moche. De este modo, las escenas pueden representar esfuerzos a favor de los centros costeros huaca para consolidar el poder y mantener la estabilidad entre poblaciones potencialmente rebeldes.

Mucho del trabajo artístico moche pudo haber sido de naturaleza ideológica. Las creencias fundamentales acerca de la vida, muerte y regeneración y la organización del cosmos pudieron haber sido maleables y sujetas a manipulación al servicio de fines sociopolíticos. Al emplear en el arte metáforas pertenecientes al cuerpo humano y al amplio cosmos, los moches estaban efectivamente insertando y naturalizando su ideología dentro de procesos que podrían ser ampliamente entendidos por sus espectadores intencionales.

Contents

List of Illustrations

(All illustrations by Andrew Turner, unless otherwise noted in caption)

Chapter 1:
Introduction

The Moche art style is best known through its highly refined ceramic vessels, which frequently accompanied burials. Estimates suggest that there are over 100,000 Moche vessels in museum and private collections worldwide (Donnan 1976: 13). The vessels, often decorated in a strongly pictorial style uncharacteristic of art of the Central Andean region, offer modern viewers tantalizing glimpses of Moche worldview. The highly consistent and formalized iconography on Moche vessels has been the topic of numerous studies, beginning around the middle of the last century, which have shed light on important aspects of Moche society such as mythology, social organization, and ceremonialism. A particularly confounding subset of Moche ceramics portrays figures, including deities, skeletal beings, humans and animals, engaged in sexual acts. While such vessels inevitably arouse the interest of modern museum visitors, to date, relatively few scholarly studies have investigated the emic meanings of Moche sexual vessels and the artistic intent behind their creation. This study focuses on portrayals of an often-depicted Moche deity who, in this instance, copulates with a woman (figure 1.1), and argues that such images drew upon widespread beliefs concerning the functions of a vital cosmos to make potent ideological claims of legitimacy in a richly metaphorical visual language.

"Moche" (also known as "Mochica") is the name applied to an archaeological culture dating from roughly AD 200 to 900 (Koons and Alex 2014; see Appendices 1 and 2) that flourished on ancient Peru's arid North Coast between the Chira and Huarmey river valleys (figure 1.2).[1] The Moche built large ceremonial centers, known today as *huacas*, that served as centers of artistic production, religious observation, and burial for Moche elite (Quilter 2002: 175-176).[2] Of known ceramic vessels, an estimated 95% were looted, depriving investigators of valuable contextual information that might give greater clues to their place of manufacture, distribution, and function (Donnan and McClelland 1999: 18). Moche non-utilitarian vessels were typically mold-made, and were often decorated with low relief and slip-painted scenes and designs, and sculptural appliqués. Geometric designs, portraiture, and portrayals of supernatural events and beings, warriors engaged in combat, plants and animals, captives, and architectural structures are among the subjects favored by Moche artists. Quotidian activities are seldom, if ever, portrayed in Moche art (Donnan 1976: 130-136).

The primary focus of this study, a mold-made neck jar with a globular body from the Museo Larco (ML004365) (figure 1.1), is one of ten documented vessels (nine executed in low-relief, and one painted in fine-line slip; see Appendix 3) that depict scenes on the body of the vessel involving a fanged deity who copulates with a woman within an architectural structure. The deity is commonly referred to by scholars as "Wrinkle Face," and has distinctive features including a belt that terminates in the head of a serpent, serpent ear ornaments, and a headdress in the form of a feline.[3] Anthropomorphized birds and a reptile flank the structure that houses the couple in examples of the copulation scene, and two women usually stand within a separate structure. Two additional Moche ceramic vessels depict a scene in which Wrinkle Face couples with a woman beneath a tree, and three sculptural vessels portray only the amorous deity and woman in three dimensions and devoid of additional figures and objects (figure 1.3). Given that fifteen known examples of this genre survive, the representation of the sexuality of deities was apparently not an inappropriate subject for depiction in Moche art, although the deity's phallus is never explicitly shown, as in examples that portray ostensibly human figures engaged in sexual activities.

---

[1] The name "Moche" derives from the Moche Valley, which, along with the Chicama Valley, is considered to be the Moche "heartland." "Mochica" is based on Muchic, a language spoken on the north coast at the time of the Spanish Conquest. Most scholars currently favor the name Moche, because it is unknown whether or not the peoples associated with the archaeological culture spoke Muchic.

[2] The Quechua term "huaca" refers more generally to a quality of sacrality, and can refer to a location, object, or being.

[2] The Quechua term "huaca" refers more generally to a quality of sacrality, and can refer to a location, object, or being.

[3] Wrinkle Face is also occasionally referred to as Aipaec ("the Creator"

---

[3] Wrinkle Face is also occasionally referred to as Aipaec ("the Creator" in Muchic), Quismique ("Old One"), God A, God F, the Fanged God, and the Serpent Belt God. I do not use the name Aipaec because it is not clear that the Moche viewed the deity in question as a creator or supreme deity, or that they spoke Muchic. A number of supernatural beings in Moche art have fangs, so "Fanged God" provides little clarification. I prefer the term "Wrinkle Face" because it refers to one of his most distinctive features without imposing or assuming additional traits.

Figure 1.1. Jar with low-relief copulation scene. Museo Larco, Lima. ML004365.

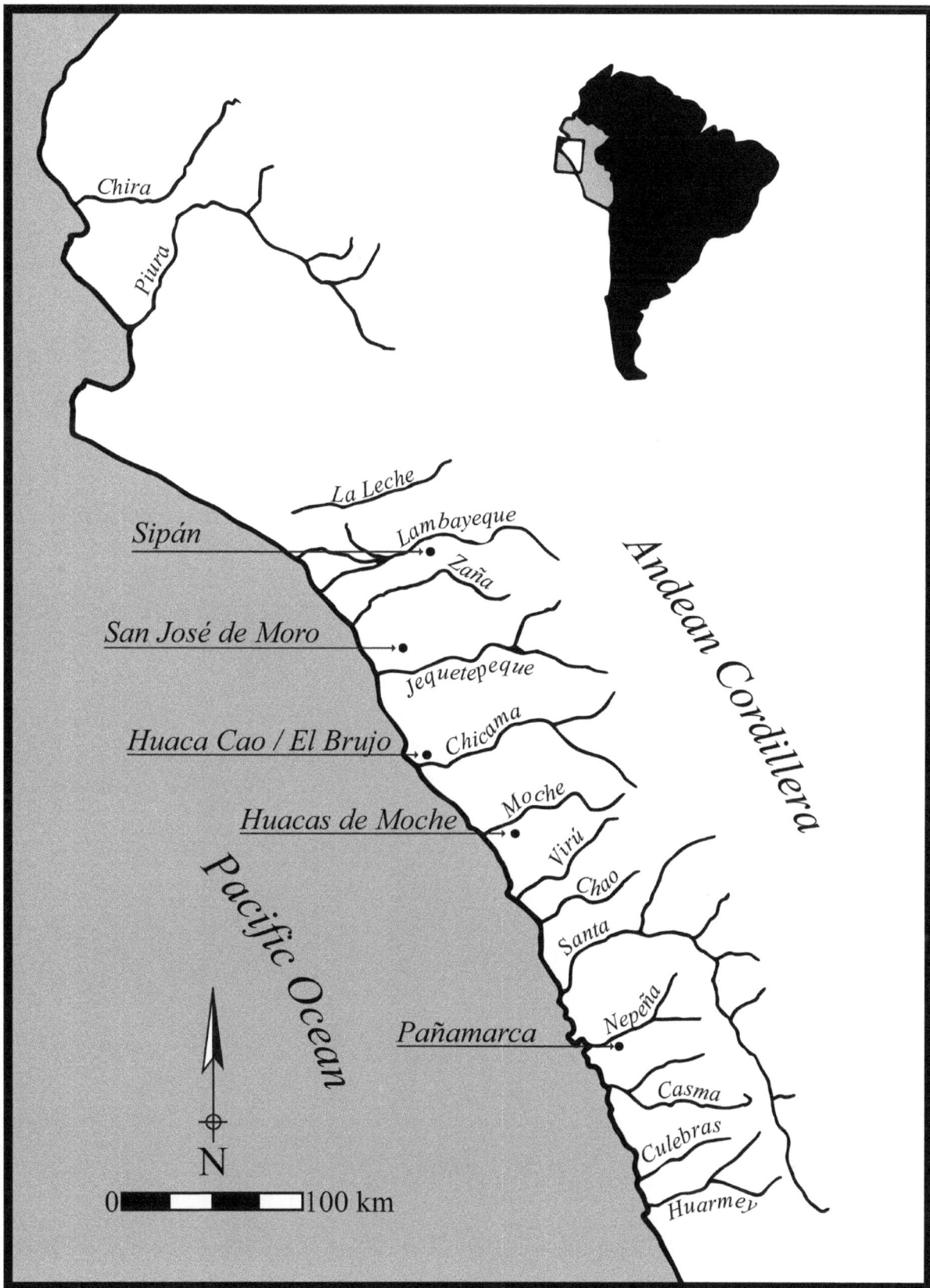

Figure 1.2. Map of the Moche region showing major sites and river valleys. Drawing by author and Eric Heller.

Figure 1.3. Jar representing figures embracing. Museo Larco, Lima.

Ceramic vessels portraying sexual acts are also known in smaller numbers from archaeological cultures such as Vicús, Salinar, Gallinazo, Recuay, Nasca, Lima, Casma, Lambayeque, Wari and Chimú, but the largest corpus is by far that of the Moche. A total of at least 500 Moche ceramic vessels are known which display sexually explicit imagery, not including vessels portraying "war captives with exposed genitalia, dancing skeletons with erect penises, and vessels with highly suggestive motifs and forms" (Weismantel 2004: 495). Estimates suggest that less than 1% of Moche ceramics are classifiable as sexually explicit or suggestive in nature, and almost all non-looted examples were recovered in funerary contexts (Gebhard 1970: 118). The age and sex of the deceased do not seem to have dictated the presence or absence of sexually explicit vessels as mortuary offerings in Moche tombs (Gebhard 1970: 118; Larco Hoyle 1965: 44). Despite the relative paucity of sexual depictions in Moche vessels, the subset is worthy of attention, given the general lack of portrayals of sexual intercourse in the art of the ancient Americas and the opportunity it affords to investigate Moche attitudes and beliefs revolving around sexuality and related concepts.

The function of decorated Moche ceramic vessels remains a topic of debate among scholars, although it is a crucial to understand the intended uses of such vessels and the contexts in which one may encounter them in order to adequately comprehend the imagery and meaning that they convey. One particular type, the stirrup-spout vessel (figure 1.4), which consists of a globular body from which two tubes emerge and join together to make a central spout, was produced by coastal cultures for more than two millennia, beginning with the Cupisnique culture of the Early Horizon, and ending on Peru's North Coast around the end of the Late Horizon. The form itself was likely considered iconic, and the failure of the vessel type to survive Spanish colonialism suggests that it may have held religious significance or usage that was not in step with Christian beliefs, at least for Contact-era Chimú-Inca. The spout, which conjoins two streams of liquid when the vessel is poured, may exemplify the Andean concept of *tinkuy* (Quilter 2010: 43), a pervasive notion that the joining of two opposed forces, such as streams of liquid or rivers, is a highly significant, spiritually charged event. As such, it is conceivable that stirrup-spout vessels were used in rituals that involved the pouring of liquid offerings.

Figure 1.4. Stirrup-spout vessel.
Museo Larco, Lima.

In addition to stirrup-spout vessels, low relief and detailed slip-painted imagery referred to as "fine-line" appear on a variety of specialized ceramic vessel forms. The spout-and-handle vessel may be derived from the stirrup-spout vessel, and consists of a globular body, ring base, a straight, tubular spout that emerges from the top of the chamber, and a curved tubular handle that attaches the side of the spout to the body. Spout-and-handle vessels are more common in later Moche phases. Neck jars have globular bodies similar to that of the stirrup-spout vessel and spout-and-handle vessel, but have wide, flaring mouths (see figure 1.1). Conical flaring vessels, known as *floreros*, may also be decorated with imagery, either around the inner rim or on the sides. Sculptural effigy vessels can take the form of a variety of subjects, including deities, humans, animals, vegetables, buildings, costume elements, or elaborate tableaux, and frequently have an attached stirrup spout or spout and handle assembly.

Excavated Moche fine wares occur in funerary assemblages, leading some scholars (e.g. Bourget 2006: 48-49; Tello *et al.* 2003: 175) to believe that they were not manufactured for uses other than to be placed as grave offerings. Donnan and McClelland (1999: 18-19) argue that most vessels show signs of abrasion, chipping, and repair, and were therefore not manufactured as grave goods and may have had a variety of other uses (also Donnan 1976: 65; 1992: 119). Other scholars consider the vessels to have had limited use in ceremonial activity, but to have been used primarily in funerary rituals (Rengifo Chunga and Rojas Vega 2008: 333; Russell and Jackson 2001: 168; Uceda and Armas 1998: 108). In regard to stirrup-spout vessels, Quilter (2002: 164-165) suggests that they were prized for their symbolic value, individualism, and imagery over their utilitarian value. Given that such vessels appear in high-status burials, are carefully decorated with religious themes and imagery, and were produced at huaca centers rather than in domestic contexts, I do not consider them to be utilitarian in nature, but rather as important ritual objects that were likely used in ceremonies and possibly feasting, but were ultimately destined to accompany the deceased.

Among Moche ceramics that represent humans engaged in sex acts, characters involved are typically rendered as freestanding three-dimensional "deck figures" on top of vessel chambers. They generally have expressionless faces, and do not belong to narrative scenes that include other characters or specific contextualizing objects (figure 1.5).[4] Curiously, a variety of sexual acts and positions are represented, but vaginal sex is rare and methods that would not lead to pregnancy are most commonly portrayed, including oral sex, masturbation and, most frequently, anal sex. Genitalia of both sexes are rendered in careful anatomical detail, and phalli are often exaggerated in scale. Men are typically dressed in tunics and head cloths, and women are most frequently nude with the occasional exception of a collar, and have long braids. Despite claims to the contrary (e.g. Arboleda 1981; Gebhard 1970: 127; Kauffmann-Doig 1979: 46-48; Mathieu 2003: 35), there are as yet no confirmed authentic representations of homosexual intercourse, and oft-cited examples appear to be modern forgeries. In several instances, humans engage in sexual acts with skeletal beings. Animals, such as llamas and mice, are also occasionally portrayed engaged in copulation.

Figure 1.5. Stirrup-spout vessel with copulating deck figures. Museo Larco, Lima. ML004253.

Although the term "erotic" is commonly used to describe Andean vessels that portray sexual behavior, I avoid usage of this adjective to describe Moche examples. The term carries connotations of sexual arousal and titillation, and it is by no means apparent that Moche vessels were intended to elicit such responses in the viewers for whom they were produced. Attitudes toward sex and reproduction are highly variable in different cultural and social contexts, and it is therefore necessary to avoid assumptions that modern Western notions of sexuality are universal, especially in considering cultures known purely through the archaeological record.

Previous scholarly works have approached sexually explicit Moche vessels in a variety of ways. Gebhard (1970), whose investigations were supported by the Kinsey Institute, approached the vessels as a representational catalog of the sexual practices of the Moche people. A number of authors have viewed them as didactic objects intended to demonstrate methods of contraception (Cáceres Macedo 2000: 34; Jiménez Borja 1985: 44; Kauffmann-Doig 1979: 38; Larco Hoyle 1965). Larco Hoyle (1965: 87, 89) considered certain vessels that portray skeletons engaged in sex acts as objects that convey moralizing content,

---

[4] An exception is the frequent inclusion of an infant that suckles at its mother's breast as she lies partially covered by a blanket and is penetrated anally by a crouching male figure. See Weismantel 2004.

demonstrating the degenerating effects of certain sexual behaviors. Several studies (Benson 1972: 146-148; Bergh 1993; Gebhard 1970: 129-131; Kauffmann-Doig 1979: 87; Larco Hoyle 1965: 81; Mathieu 2003: 31) have explored the possibility that Moche vessels convey sexual humor. Others (Benson 1972: 148-151; Bourget 2006; Dobkin de Rios 1977: 199; Donnan 1976: 133-134, 1982: 101; Gero 2004: 19; Hocquenghem 1989: 138-139) consider sexual representations to be portrayals of ritualized or ceremonial acts.

This study does not aim at an overarching or inclusive interpretation of Moche depictions of sexual intercourse. No single explanation adequately accounts for all types of vessels that portray sexual activity, and it is therefore necessary to examine smaller subsets of thematically related imagery on their own terms in order to attempt a meaningful interpretation. Depictions of the deity Wrinkle Face engaged in sexual acts are fundamentally different from representations of copulating humans because they show a distinctive and identifiable mythical being (rather than unidentifiable or generalized human figures), they are usually part of larger scenes which strongly suggests a narrative structure, and they presumably portray vaginal intercourse based on the bodily orientation of the two participants, although genitalia are not clearly visible.[5]

Having discussed the possible functions of vessels upon which sexual imagery appears and given a brief overview of previous scholarship devoted to the subject, in Part 2 of this study, I discuss the general characteristics and nature of the Moche art style, as well as prominent methodologies for the interpretation of Moche imagery. Moche art differs in execution from other well-known art styles of the ancient Andes, and is often considered to be less "abstract" or "conceptual." After the discovery of burials interred with accouterments resembling those of beings that appear in Moche artwork, scholars have tended to view scenes involving supernatural beings as images of human actors engaged in ceremonies involving deity impersonation. While deity impersonation was likely an important component of Moche

ceremonialism, approaching Moche artwork as a record of past events may overlook the messages and motivations behind certain forms of artistic production. As a basis for iconographic interpretation in subsequent chapters, I suggest that Moche artwork was in fact rich in metaphor and draws deeply from underlying themes found in other Andean traditions.

Part 3 of this study argues that the Larco Jar and other similar vessels bearing Wrinkle Face copulation scenes were produced in a workshop in the "urban sector" of the site of Huacas de Moche. I further discuss Moche ceramic chronology and current views of Moche socio-political organization, as well as the techniques employed by Moche potters who produced mold-made ceramics. In addition to the social status of the potter and the possible functions of artistic production at huaca centers, I explore the relationship between secular and religious powers that may have shaped the southern Moche region.

In Part 4, I present an iconographic analysis of the Larco Jar and other vessels that portray Wrinkle Face copulating with a woman inside a structure. I consider the scenes to be mythological in content, and discuss the narrative sequence of events on the vessels and analyze the characters represented and other contexts in which they appear. Drawing upon ethnohistoric and ethnographic accounts, I relate the scenes to widespread Andean conceptions regarding the circulation of fluids and the relationship of the human body to the larger cosmos and its functions.

Part 5 explores the relationship between scenes in which Wrinkle Face copulates within a house, such as on the Larco Jar, and an analogous pair of scenes in which a tree emerges from the back of Wrinkle Face during his sexual encounter with a woman. I conclude that the images depict Wrinkle Face as a paramount ancestor, a role linked to both human and agricultural fertility in a number of Andean belief systems, and this interpretation supports Benson's (1997a: 45, 2012: 69) proposal that Wrinkle Face copulation scenes may represent an origin myth for the Moche people. In constructing this argument, I consider Moche notions of materiality as well as Andean funerary customs and beliefs concerning death. My contention is that Moche artists, or perhaps more accurately those under whose patronage they worked, manipulated existing mythological and cosmological beliefs to suit the ideological aims of huaca centers like Huacas de Moche.

---

[5] One sculptural example, a stirrup-spout vessel at the Museo Larco (ML004211) in which Wrinkle Face and his consort appear as deck figures does portray anal sex, although it stands in contrast to other examples, as he penetrates her from behind, rather than copulating face-to-face, and he grasps her chin with his right hand, a gesture that sometimes occurs in examples showing couples in Moche, Casma, and Chimú vessels. The gesture also occurs in Moche combat scenes in which a triumphant warrior grasps the chin of a captive.

Analysis of the Larco Jar that depicts the deity Wrinkle Face copulating with an anthropomorphic female (figure 1.1) suggests that Moche artists made abundant use of metaphor to convey meanings in their works that are not immediately apparent to the modern eye. Moche artists and elites created artwork rich in symbolism to propagate ideologies consistent with the aims and functions of Moche religious centers. Although sexual imagery is not particularly common in the Andes, the vessels in question present themes consistent with a general substrate of Andean worldview, however these themes were manipulated to suit the requirements specific to the social, political, and physical environment in which they were produced.

Chapter 2:
Moche Art in Context

In strictly visual terms, the Moche art style is perhaps the most representational, non-abstract style in the ancient Central Andes. The surface-level legibility of Moche art is readily appealing to Western sensibilities, which tend to favor verism over abstraction, and yet, despite the approachable nature of imagery on Moche ceramics, metalwork, architectural friezes, and other media, many works are not readily comprehensible to the modern viewer. Perhaps in part, owing to the fact that Moche art is so different in appearance from most other ancient Andean art styles, scholars have generally been hesitant to interpret Moche artwork vis-à-vis broadly shared themes in the Andes. Although it differs in appearance from other Andean forms, I argue that the more "realistic" art style made wide use of metaphor, and therefore can be misleading to investigators who seek literal interpretations.

The highly pictorial quality of small-scale Moche art sets it apart from many other Andean visual systems. Moche art follows consistent rules across media (Donnan 1976: 5), and the Moche style "aims for clarity in reading" (Bock 2005: 2). In other words, the visually descriptive and detailed style employed by Moche artists seems to reflect intentions to minimize ambiguity in visual representation. In contrast to the relatively static representations of deities, humans, and animals in the artwork of other Andean cultures such as Chavín, Nasca, Wari and Tiwanaku, Moche pottery painting and low relief vessel decoration focus on action, movement, and interaction between figures. Characters are often placed in detailed scenes, and artists frequently used techniques such as scale and vertical positioning to indicate depth of field (Donnan 1976: 23, 24), and "locators" to denote various physical environments (Donnan and McClelland 1999: 59). In figure 2.1, the artist has employed vertical positioning by placing dunes or hills and plants in the upper portion of the scene in order to provide a sense of depth in the image. *Tillandsia*, a genus of epiphytic plants that grows in the arid coastal *lomas* of Peru, and cacti are provided as "locators" that indicate that the scene is set in the desert. Furthermore, a series of Moche portrait vessels is one of the few corpuses in the Andes that can be considered portraiture in the

Western sense, capturing individualized visible likeness of the subject (see Donnan 2004).

The Moche style is a departure from the earlier traditions. The widespread Chavín style of the Early Horizon widely makes use of devices such as symmetry, anatropic (reversible) imagery (Kubler 1962: 242), contour rivalry (Burger 1992: 147-148), and the metaphorical substitutions or transformation of parts of figures into other forms referred to as "kenning" (Rowe 1967). "Kenning" is visible in the transformation of the hair and belt of the frontally facing Chavín supernatural being illustrated in figure 2.2 into serpents. Generally lacking such stylistic conventions, or at least not using them to the extent that prior art styles did, the descriptive nature of Moche art may be a demystification of earlier, more esoteric religious traditions (Quilter 2001: 40).

It is noteworthy that the art style found on portable Moche objects, such as bodily ornaments, ceremonial accouterments, and ceramic vessels, often differs from the style visible on "public" façades of monumental architecture, which more closely resembles that of other Andean traditions. Imagery on ceramic vessels, especially in later phases, is generally more detailed and energetic, whereas the highly visible murals of ceremonial structures such as Huaca de la Luna (figure 2.3) and Huaca Cao Viejo tend to portray regularized and geometricized figures and repeated patterns. The stylized, repetitive friezes of the aforementioned sites appear to draw inspiration from woven textile design. Certain motifs represented in murals, such as spiders and frontally depicted deities, recall the art of earlier traditions such as Chavín and Cupisnique. Moche monumental artwork served as a luxurious and otherworldly backdrop for public spectacle, and likely achieved legitimacy through a sense of grandeur and reference to the past. By contrast, the fluid and figural imagery on ceramics was novel and does not appear to be plectogenetic in nature. The more didactic style used on portable objects was not intended for mass consumption or public spectacle, but rather was produced for more private viewing and was likely oriented toward and consumed by more exclusive social strata.

*Figure 2.1. Rollout drawing of Moche fine-line scene depicting depth of field and "locators."
After drawing by Donna McClelland.*

Figure 2.2. Relief-carved block, Chavín de Huantar, Early Horizon.

Figure 2.3. Mural painting, east sector of Ceremonial Patio, Huaca de la Luna.

Figure 2.4. Rollout drawing of fine-line Presentation Theme scene.
After drawing by Donna McClelland.

Discussions of the conceptual nature of Andean art typically exclude the Moche style. While twentieth-century collectors were attracted to densely pictorial prehispanic art styles such as Moche and Maya, Modernists favored prehispanic art that emphasized form and apparently lacked complex iconography because it could be experienced unmediated (Pasztory 1997: 65). Well-known examples of Andean conceptualism include the Nasca lines, which cannot be viewed as recognizable forms as they were experienced by people at ground-level, Wari textiles which exhibit varying degrees of geometric abstraction, and Inca stonework and sculpture, which is characterized as abstract (D'Harnoncourt 1954: 14) or "presentational," rather than representational (Dean 2006a). Scholars point to the primacy of the medium of weaving as a point of departure for works in other media and as the basis of Andean conceptualism (Paternosto 1996: 18), since a woven object must be planned in its entirety before beginning (Pasztory 1997: 63)

Donnan (1976) argued that Moche art was a highly symbolic system, and Moche artists did not seek to represent aspects of daily life. Even depictions in artwork of seemingly quotidian activities such as weaving and the production of *chicha* (maize beer) were charged with additional "non-secular" meaning beyond the physical tasks they represent. According to Donnan, who compared Moche art to ethnohistoric accounts and modern shamanistic beliefs and practices, Moche imagery was imbued with ceremonialism, and a major focus was the depiction of ritual activity. For Donnan, Moche art provided a window into the spiritual beliefs and ritual lives of practitioners of Moche religion, rather

than a documentary glimpse of the everyday lives of Moche people.

Beginning in the 1970s, scholars began to seek methodological approaches to aid in the interpretation of Moche iconography. Donnan (1976: 117, 1977: 407) noted that Moche artwork could be broken down into a relatively small number of "themes." His Thematic Approach attempts to systematically identify themes and isolate their constituent elements. Themes represented in painted scenes on Moche pottery and other media described by Donnan include the Presentation Theme (figure 2.4), which involves the sacrifice of captives and the presentation of their blood in a goblet to a rayed figure (Donnan 1976: 117-129, 1977), and the Burial Theme, which involves several activities undertaken by Wrinkle Face (the same deity represented on the vessel that is the object of this study) and his reptilian companion, Iguana, including the burial of a casket and the presentation of conch shells to a kneeling figure (Donnan and McClelland 1979). Moche artists could depict a theme through individual symbolic units or through combinations of multiple elements (Donnan 1977: 419). For example, Moche artists could represent a Presentation Theme scene in its entirety or, relying on the viewer's prior understanding of the theme, artists could rather portray one or two elements, such as the sacrifice of captives, and thus allude to larger theme without showing all parts in a *pars pro toto* manner.

Arguing that the Thematic Approach led to a proliferation of identified and catalogued themes, but generally lacked explanatory capabilities,

Quilter (1997) proposed the Narrative Approach, which attempts to stitch together themes that share common elements into larger narratives. The Narrative Approach assumes that much of Moche art is based on myths that have continuities and recurring narrative patterns. Quilter notes that the boundaries between myth, ritual, and history are often blurred. Once identified, narratives can be evaluated against ethnographic and ethnohistoric sources, meaning can be approximated, and slippages in a given narrative's structure and/or constituent elements can reveal significant historical and ideological shifts.

Discoveries in the late 1980s and early 1990s at the northern Moche sites of Sipán (see Alva and Donnan 1993) and San José de Moro (see Donnan and Castillo 1992) changed the ways that scholars approach Moche art. Both sites yielded sumptuous burials of high-status individuals with costumes and accouterments similar to those worn by characters depicted in the Presentation Theme. Presumably, the elites buried within the tombs ritually enacted the sacrificial event portrayed in a series of Moche vessels. The discovery of people inhumed with accouterments similar to those of characters appearing in Moche art has complicated rather than resolved interpretation, and has led scholars, perhaps falsely, to view representation in Moche art as a window into social practices (Quilter 2002: 162-166). A recent trend has been to focus on Moche scenes as representations of ritual events or ceremonies based on myths, rather than as primarily mythological in content (e.g. Bourget 2006: 48; Hocquenghem 1989: 23). The shift in emphasis away from viewing Moche art as a system rich in symbolism and mythical in subject matter toward an approach that considers Moche representations as historical documents that catalog social events widens the presumed rift in conceptuality between Moche art and that of other ancient Andean cultures. Recent studies have tended to downplay the role of metaphor in both ceremony and artwork.

This study argues that while Moche artists made use of narrative in their works, it was not at the expense of metaphor, and metaphor was a primary vehicle for conveying meaning in Moche visual culture. Metaphor can be defined as "a move from a whole to one of its parts to another whole which contains that part, or from a member to a general class and then back again to a member of that class" (Tilley 1999: 4). Given the arbitrary relationship between objects, concepts, and events and the words and signs used to describe them (Saussure 1983), metaphors are necessary components of human language and serve as a basis for understanding the world through analogic thinking, which is mediated through bodily experience (Tilley 1999). The human body served as the apparatus for understanding the world and as the basic form from which to draw analogies, and like other Andean cultures, the cosmos and its functions were understood through a series of bodily metaphors. Human sexuality was thus linked to larger-scale phenomena such as social organization and agricultural fertility. Moche elites manipulated these understandings to promote certain ideologies that were rendered in intransient visual form through mold-made ceramic works such as the Larco Jar.

Chapter 3:
Ceramic Production and the Distribution of Power

Although the conditions under which the Larco Jar was unearthed are unknown and it was not found during a documented, systematic excavation, it is nonetheless possible to approximate the date and location of its manufacture. Based on analysis of its form, style, and method of production, the jar was likely produced in a workshop at the site of Huacas de Moche (also known as Moche or Huacas del Sol y de la Luna), located in the Moche Valley near the modern city of Trujillo. According to Larco Hoyle's five-phase chronology of Moche vessel forms (1948), the jar belongs to Phase IV, when Huacas de Moche reached its apogee. Examination of Moche pottery production and the role of huaca centers also sheds light on the social conditions and motives behind the creation of the vessel.

The phenomenon that we understand as "Moche" was regionally variable, and changed through time. For most of the twentieth century, Moche was considered the first expansionist state in the Andes, but that notion has recently been subject to serious scrutiny (e.g. Quilter and Koons 2012). Scholars now recognize Moche as at least two or more distinct political units that shared a common art style and ideology (Castillo 2001: 307; Quilter 2002: 160-161). A broad distinction can be made between northern and southern Moche regions, separated by an extensive tract of desert between the Chicama and Jequetepeque valleys known as the Pampa de Paiján. In actuality, there were probably several unique localized iterations of the Moche phenomenon, and therefore broad generalizations and homogenizing statements about the Moche as a whole are misleading (Quilter 2010) and assumptions that the purpose of Moche art was unvaried throughout the 700-year duration of the phenomenon are problematic (Quilter 2002: 166). Furthermore, the modern conception of the Moche phenomenon may not have been recognized as valid by the people associated with the remains (Quilter 2002: 155). In all likelihood, Moche served as a suite of traditions that linked elites from various polities together in social, economical, and technological exchange (Castillo B. and Quilter 2010: 15), and the phenomenon may have cross-cut ethnic or linguistic barriers. Moche traits can be understood as a collection of "symbols of dominant religious and political ideology, serving the interests of a ruling elite" (Bawden 1996: 8), rather than as byproducts of a monolithic culture.

Ceramics have served as the primary basis for marking cultural and chronological change in the Moche region and across the Andes. In a highly influential study, Larco Hoyle (1948) divided Moche chronology into five phases based on ceramic vessel form and spout morphology, especially that of stirrup-spout vessels. Larco's sequence reflects his belief that the Moche were controlled by a single centralized political entity (Castillo B. and Quilter 2010: 10; Koons and Alex 2014: 1040). It has generally been assumed that each phase lasted 100 to 200 years, and his chronology suggests a gradual unilinear evolutionary model of cultural change. While Larco's sequence has been useful in the south, it has become increasingly apparent that it is not effective in the northern Moche region (Benson 2012: 7; Castillo B. and Quilter 2010: 11-13; Chapdelaine 2011; McClelland, *et al.* 2007: 7; Quilter 2002: 160). Furthermore, Lockard (2008, 2009) has demonstrated that there is significant chronological overlap between the production of Moche IV and Moche V ceramics in the Moche Valley, and Koons and Alex (2014) note that, as the two styles are contemporary in some regions, the distinction between Moche IV and Moche V is likely more ideological than chronological.

Donnan (2011) has recently proposed that Larco's chronology may be more a reflection of the deliberate creation of local sub-styles by different polities, than one of temporal change along a linear evolutionary continuum. Donnan (2011) proposes four distinct sub-styles that were linked, respectively, to the sites of San José de Moro, Dos Cabezas, Huancaco, and Huacas de Moche as major production centers. The Huacas de Moche sub-style was the largest, and was distributed over most of the southern Moche region, including the Moche, Chicama, Virú, Chao, and Santa valleys (Donnan 2011: 117). Although Donnan's proposal implies that the various "phases" of Moche pottery are less a byproduct of a homogenous and steady stylistic progression over time and more the result of the proliferation and distribution of works from specific workshops or groups of workshops, a given sub-style does represent a bounded nexus of time and location, as production and distribution were spatially and temporally related to the duration of producing workshops and the proliferation and desirability of their products. Phase IV may in fact be synonymous with a fully developed and widely distributed Huacas de Moche sub-style, although further assessment and consideration of the implications for earlier phases are necessary.

Examining the methods used to produce the Larco Jar and vessels bearing similar imagery provides further evidence of its origin. Moche vessels were frequently made using complex molding techniques (Donnan 1965: 117-119; Russell and Jackson 2001: 169). An unprovenanced ceramic object at the Museo Larco (figure 2.1) is typically described as a bowl (e.g. Cáceres Macedo 2000: 61); however, displayed as a bowl, the low-relief imagery is upside-down. Upon closer examination of the object and in consideration of mold-making processes, it is apparent that the object is not a bowl, but likely served as a matrix from which a ceramic mold was made. Molds and matrices are rare, because they don't typically appear in funerary assemblages (Donnan 1965: 118), they are less attractive to collectors, and they were subject to wear and tear that probably most often resulted in their destruction (Mowat 1988: 4). Furthermore, they were often made of unfired clay, which may also contribute to their scarcity in the archaeological record (Mowat 1988: 5). The imagery on the matrix is nearly identical to that of the molded low-relief scene on the Larco Jar, and while it was not the very matrix from which the vessel in question was made, it was nonetheless likely produced in the same workshop, based on their strong similarities in style, execution, parent clay, and subject matter, and it provides insight into the production methods and conditions in which the Larco Jar was made.

Close inspection of a spout-and-handle vessel, also in the collection of the Museo Larco, suggests that it was made from a mold taken from the matrix (figure 2.2). The features, proportions, and minute imperfections of the two objects are identical. Although the spout-and-handle vessel is significantly smaller than the matrix, the difference in size is accountable through consideration of the mold-making process. When wet clay was placed on the matrix to make the mold, it shrunk as the moisture evaporated. Wet clay that was later pressed into the mold to make a vessel then shrunk further as it dried. Thus, the size of the cast vessel is twice reduced from the size of the matrix. The aperture of the matrix was left open so that the potter could press clay into the mold. A ring base was attached to the cast vessel after removal from the mold, and in this case, the artist added a hand-built handle and spout.

Thompson (1963) described a Middle Horizon or Late Intermediate period matrix from the Huarmey Valley. Like the Moche matrix, the bottom was left open, and an incised line bisects the object, although Thompson believed that the line served as a guide for forming the two halves of the mold independently. This explanation seems unlikely, because making two clay mold-halves at different stages increases the likelihood that they will not join properly due to differential shrinkage from inconsistent moisture content in the wet clay, thus leaving an off-set on the seam-line of the cast that would require additional work to repair with each subsequent pull from the mold. The mold-making method employed by Moche artists insured that little trace of a seam-line could be detected in the finished cast, as in the Larco Jar. At least two different molds were made from the Larco Matrix. Straight incisions that bisect it (figure 2.3) indicate that it was completely covered in wet clay and then as the clay shell hardened, it was cut in half to make a two-piece mold. Another two-piece mold was produced from the matrix, but it was cut on a different axis. The visible incisions indicate that the matrix was unfired at the time the molds were made. At some point after the molds were made, the matrix was burnished. The detail in the highest relief was obliterated or smoothed, and the portions of the incised lines made while cutting the molds were also burnished out. The matrix was later fired, and was perhaps then used as a bowl or cup in the workshop after it was no longer useful for making molds.

The potter that made the matrix left the top as an undecorated field for the attachment of the spout. In the case of the copy made from its mold, incisions were poked through the wall of the vessel so that the chamber could be filled and emptied with liquid, and a spout and handle were attached. The blank field at the top of the globular vessel body could also accommodate a variety of different hand-built spout types, including a stirrup spout, or a jar neck, as in the case of the Larco Jar. This modularity in spout shape is significant, because it suggests that although the imagery in question only occurs on globular vessels, it is not specific to a particular type of globular vessel. The matrix could produce a variety of vessel types, and indeed scenes portraying Wrinkle Face engaged in copulation appear on a jar, spout-and-handle vessels, or stirrup-spout vessels.[6] The potter could perhaps select the

---

[6] Of the ten known examples bearing this scene, at least one is a stirrup-spout vessel, and three are spout-and-handle vessels.

Figure 3.1. Probable mold matrix with low-relief copulation scene.
Museo Larco, Lima. ML004363.

Figure 3.2. Spout-and-handle vessel with low-relief copulation scene (ML004361) and the
probable mold matrix from which it was made (ML004363). Museo Larco, Lima.

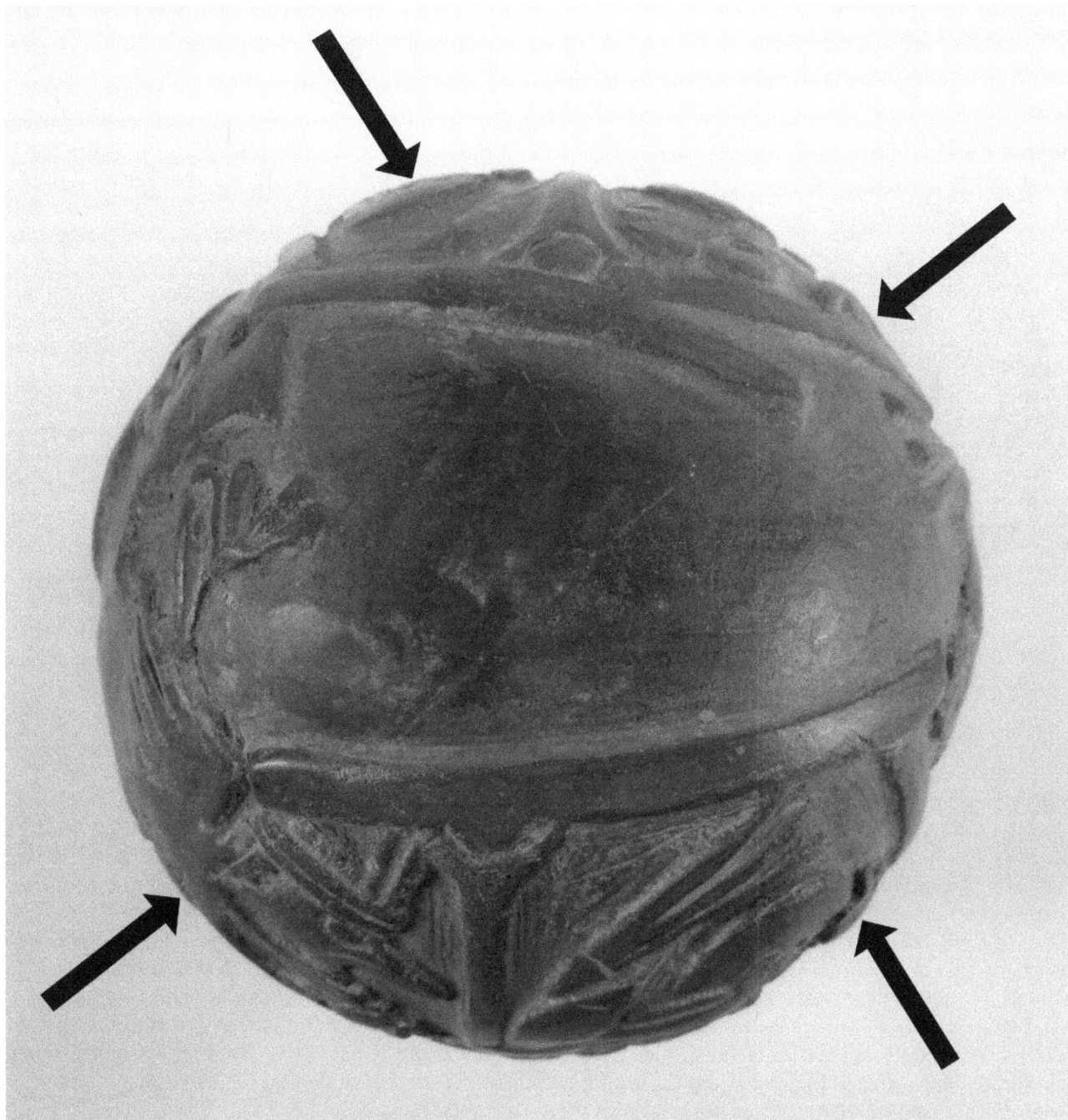

Figure 3.3. Probable mold matrix with low-relief copulation scene (top view).
Incised lines are indicated by arrows. Museo Larco, Lima. ML004363.

type of vessel upon which the scene would appear, or could accommodate the requirements of different patrons or different intended uses of the vessels produced from a single matrix.

Figure 3.4. Jar from Huaca de la Luna, Plaza 1. After drawing by Jorge Sachún.

Although the scene on the body of the Larco Jar is slightly different from the matrix and spout-and-handle vessel in terms of the proportions and relative placement of figures, it appears to be identical or nearly identical to the illustration of a jar excavated at Huacas de Moche (figure 2.4). The jar was found in an intrusive female burial dating to around AD 600 in the northeastern corner of Plaza 1 of Huaca de la Luna, along with twenty-one other vessels (Chapdelaine 2001: 80-81). The strong similarities between the Larco Jar and the example from Plaza 1 suggest that they were produced in the same workshop, or likely from the same mold.

The form, production methods, and imagery on the Larco Jar and its possible duplicate found in the Plaza 1 burial dating to AD 600 are consistent with other vessels that constitute the Phase IV (or Huacas de Moche) sub-style. Decorated spout-and-handle vessels also first appeared in Phase IV (Donnan and McClelland 1999: 80), and sexual scenes involving Wrinkle Face are seemingly limited in distribution to Phase IV and the southern Moche region. In

general, Phase IV ceramics are rare in the northern region (Benson 1997a: 41). Phase IV shows the most evidence of mass-production (Donnan 1965: 128), and in Phases IV and V, painted and low-relief narrative scenes become more common than the isolated sculpted or painted figures and designs prevalent in Phases I through III. Donnan (1976: 62) attributes an increased complexity in visual representation apparent in later Moche phases to more diverse and sophisticated artistic developments, but Quilter (1997: 130) suggests that a move toward narration in Late Moche art was ideological in nature, and may have involved a shift toward "objectivity," narrativity, and a greater tendency toward moralizing in mythology. Recent calibrated carbon dates at Huacas de Moche place Phase IV between AD 400 and 700 (Chapdelaine 2001: 73), which corresponds to the apogee and decline of Huacas de Moche.

Investigation of the workshop in which the Larco Jar was likely produced suggests that part of the function of huaca centers appears to have been the production of high-status objects and goods associated with ritual or ceremonial use. Uceda's excavations in the urban zone located between the Huaca de la Luna and the Huaca del Sol at Huacas de Moche revealed separate compounds for textile production, a metal workshop, *chicha* production areas, and a ceramics workshop (figure 2.5). There was no evidence of the production of undecorated utilitarian vessels within the ceramics workshop (Uceda and Armas 1998: 105), which appear to have been produced elsewhere (Rengifo Chunga and Rojas Vega 2008: 327). In the 1994-1995 field season, Uceda's team found "some 1,000 whole and fragmentary molds of figurines, trumpets, stirrup-spout bottles, face-neck jars, and appliqués, and numerous matrices for making molds" in Moche's urban sector (Uceda and Armas 1998: 93). The number of matrices and molds found suggests large-scale production (Armas 1999: 67, cited in Rengifo Chunga and Rojas Vega 2008: 328). Iconographic material in the workshop included faces, prisoners, animals, fanged deities, men, women, children, and "erotic" scenes (Rengifo Chunga and Rojas Vega 2008: 328). Based on these findings, Uceda concludes that the Phase IV workshop produced goods for "elite burials and ritual activities" (Uceda and Armas 1998: 108). The workshop went through three construction phases (Rengifo Chunga and Rojas Vega 2008: 338), and was likely part of a larger potter's barrio based on similar finds outside of the compound and the distribution of manufacture materials (Rengifo Chunga and Rojas Vega 2008: 329; Uceda and Armas 1998: 107).

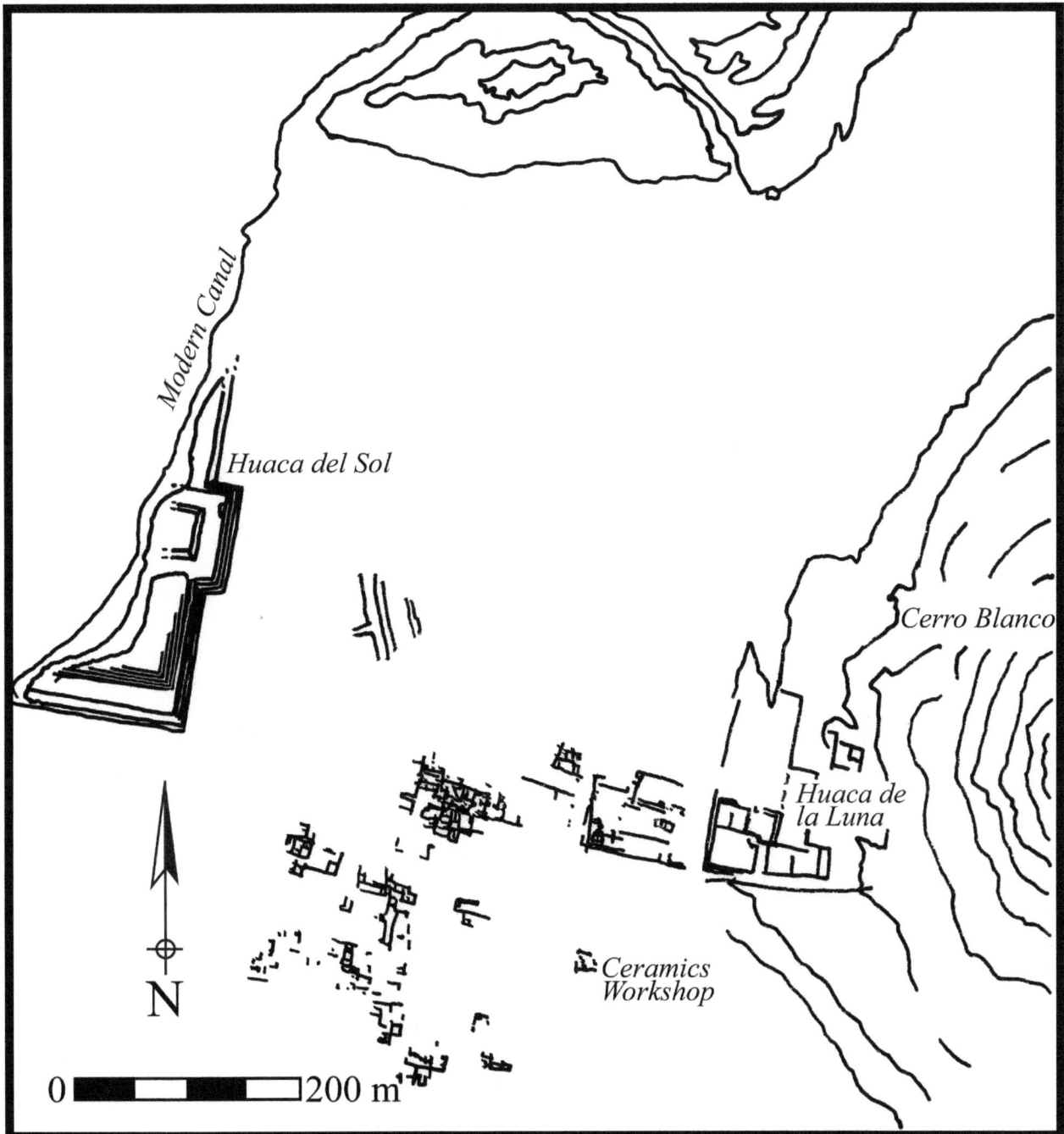

Figure 3.5. Plan of Huacas de Moche showing ceramics workshop.
Redrawn and modified after Chapdelaine 2001: fig. 1 by author and Eric Heller.

Evidence from urban zone at Cao Viejo in the Chicama Valley also suggests that it may have been a production area for funerary and ritual goods (Quilter 2002: 176-177).

Based on available evidence, the conditions of pottery production and the status of potters apparently varied throughout the Moche region (Costin 2004: 198-199; Russell, *et al.* 1998). An excavated workshop from Cerro Mayal, located in the Chicama Valley, appears to have produced specialized ceramics of medium quality for elites at nearby Mocollope (Jackson 2008: 49-53; Russell, *et al.* 1998; Russell and Jackson 2001). A Moche V workshop at Pampa Grande was located in a non-residential zone near the site's center, although the potters themselves may not have been elites (Shimada 1994: 195-197). Considering the central location of workshops in Huacas de Moche, potters and other artists may have had privileged status and an active role in the formulation of Moche ideology. According to Rengifo Chunga and Rojas Vega (2008: 337), craft specialists were likely economically, ideologically, and politically engrained in Moche society, producing high-status goods and paraphernalia and making use of and perpetuating Moche symbolism. Uceda and Armas (1998: 108) believe that the potters belonged to the Moche elite. Artists at Huacas de Moche probably had special privileges, access, and ideological knowledge, based on their important position and central location within Huacas de Moche (Rengifo Chunga and Rojas Vega 2008: 337).

Artistic production served an important function at huaca centers, although it is unclear whether artists were directly shaping Moche ideology as members of a Moche elite class, or were reflecting the needs of an elite class of which they were not a part through their artwork. The relative stability and consistency of Moche artistic rules, regardless of medium (Donnan 1976: 21) and the repetitive occurrences of themes in Moche artwork, suggest some sort of centralized control over artistic production, whether through unified guilds, or through direct orchestration from powerful elite or a priestly class. Control of ideology is linked to control of labor and economy (DeMarrais, *et al.* 1996: 18), and those in power among the Moche used materialized ideology in the form of craft production to buttress their status (Vaughn 2006). The use of molds in making ceramic vessels at on-site workshops would allow for consistency and some degree of control over the messages promoted through portable ceramics. The production of

matrices and molds required a high degree of skill and familiarity with Moche symbolism, although workers with less skill and specialized knowledge could make use of the molds during production (Costin 2004: 207; Donnan 1992: 122; Quilter 2010: 41-42).[7] Costin (2004: 211-212) notes that the Moche used varied strategies to exercise control over production. The placement of workshops within the center of Huacas de Moche and the extensive use of molds may have been effective means of controlling the content and distribution of decorated ceramics.

The precise role, function, and nature of Moche huaca centers remain poorly understood, and interpretations are often framed by Western expectations of what constitutes a city. Although the monumental architecture of Huacas de Moche was a backdrop for spectacular events including human sacrifice (Bourget 2001), it is not clear whether or not it was the primary center of political power in the Moche Valley. Evidence of palatial architecture has not been found within the site, and additional seats of political power may have been distributed throughout the countryside (Quilter 2002: 177). Furthermore, important huaca centers at the lower ends of river valleys, such as Huacas de Moche, were in a vulnerable position where they were not able to control irrigation water through force (Quilter 2002: 179, 2010: 72).

Lumbreras (1988, cited in Rengifo Chunga and Rojas Vega 2008: 326) postulated that the primary distinction between urban and rural in the Andes was the presence or absence of centers of production. Most people lived interspersed throughout the valleys (Bawden 2001: 289), residing closer to agricultural fields and other resources, and the urban zone at Huacas de Moche between the Huaca de la Luna and Huaca del Sol appears to have been foremost a production area for objects associated with ritual, and funerary goods. Quilter (2002: 175-176) suggests the possibility that religious structures at coastal huaca centers that had already been built initially attracted settlers, rather than having been built to serve the needs of a pre-existing settlement.

Huaca centers likely functioned as places of elite burial, regional mediation, and exchange for outlying communities. Unlike in previous eras,

---

[7] According to Donnan (1992: 122), by Late Moche times, more than 80% of fine wares were produced using molds.

20

Moche monumental architecture contained entombed individuals, which may have increased the sanctity of the place (Quilter 2001: 31). Although they were not elite residences, huacas did serve as temporary or permanent mortuary structures for the elite (Quilter 2002: 175). Uceda (2001: 62) believes that a source of power in Moche society was based on the veneration of ancestors, and the burial of ancestors within huacas "energized" them with their presence. The modularity of Moche adobe-block architecture, the occurrence of empty or disturbed tombs, and evidence that shows that a number of Moche skeletons found in huacas had been handled and moved prior to their ultimate burial suggests that huacas were not built to house specific deceased individuals, but rather were modified on an *ad hoc* basis, and burials were often placed within them temporarily before being moved elsewhere (Quilter 2002: 173-175). Rural elites could have thus increased their legitimacy by placing their ancestors within huacas, and huacas would then serve as pilgrimage destinations for ancestor veneration for outlying communities. As regional centers housing venerated ancestors of various local lineages, pilgrimage to huaca centers could have offered the opportunity to negotiate and resolve regional disputes, perhaps through local priests. Art objects produced at huaca centers could be exchanged with goods brought by visitors, spreading and promoting a common elite ideology and cohesiveness through a corporate art style.

As rains are sparse and infrequent on the arid coast, or catastrophic during El Niño Southern Oscillation (ENSO) events, Moche agriculturalists relied on irrigation water from rivers, streams, and canals. Although rural elites could exercise direct control over irrigation water through force, huaca centers may have expressed and maintained their power by controlling the flow of water through symbolic means. In the Andes, mountains are generally considered the source of water, and as water flows down to the coast, it is recycled back up to the mountains in a cyclical fashion (Salomon 1991: 15; Urton 1981: 60). The location of important huaca centers at the ends of river or irrigation systems may reflect a Moche belief in the concept of recycling waters from the mountains, and huaca centers may have served to invoke the flow of water through ritual (Quilter 2002: 179, 2010: 72).

During more stable times, the distribution of power may have reached a state of equilibrium through tension between rural elites who controlled resources from strategic locations, and huaca centers that controlled them from symbolic locations. Huaca centers also offered a means of legitimacy for rural elite by providing places of veneration for their deceased and by manufacturing valued art objects that conferred and buttressed their elevated status. In exchange for goods and status provided to rural lords, huaca centers likely relied on crops and raw materials brought in from the countryside. The complex relationship between secular and religious powers in Moche society is not uncommon in agrarian societies: one gaining legitimacy from the other, while both competing for power (Quilter 2002: 179). Huacas de Moche may have used the distribution of decorated pottery as a means of maintaining power.

Chapter 4:
Sex, Cosmology, and the Movement of Fluids

The imagery on the Larco Jar suggests that Moche artists created works rich in metaphor and imbued with dense, multivalent symbolism. Upon cursory examination of the vessel, the obvious focal point of the low-relief panel is the deity Wrinkle Face, who copulates with a woman in a structure, while a cast of other fantastic characters, including anthropomorphized animals, is oriented toward the pair. Other groupings of characters suggest that the scene represents a mythical narrative of sequential or simultaneous events. Closer analysis of the individual elements of the scene and how they function together as a whole links the vessel to broader Andean cosmological themes of agricultural and human fertility, and the circulation of fluids between the mountains and the coast. The vessel's imagery reflects themes central to the function of Huacas de Moche, and metaphorically links large-scale cosmological phenomena to human sexuality and the act of reproduction.

In some instances, Moche artists employed hierarchical scale to denote relative importance (Donnan 1976: 23), and Wrinkle Face and his consort are the largest figures in the scene (figure 3.1). Wrinkle Face is one of the most frequently occurring figures in Moche art, and is the only deity that appears in erotic scenes. He is generally identifiable through traits such as his striated or wrinkled face, fanged mouth, large round eyes, a fan-shaped feline headdress, serpent earrings, a tunic decorated with a stepped pattern, and a belt that terminates with serpent heads (figure 3.2). He occasionally wears a small circular nose ornament, as portrayed on the Larco Jar. Although his wrinkles and fangs are not visible, likely owing to the relative lack of fine detail possible in molded, low-relief scenes in comparison with sculpture and fine-line painting, his serpent belt and feline headdress are readily apparent. Wrinkle Face is only consistently wrinkled in Phase V depictions (Benson 2012: 61). Portrayals of Wrinkle Face begin to appear often in Phase III (Donnan and McClelland 1999: 64), and he is commonly sculpted three-dimensionally, molded in low-relief scenes, or painted in fine-line on Moche vessels.

Wrinkle Face is often accompanied by an anthropomorphic lizard, referred to as "Iguana." The pair is occasionally locked in combat against fantastic sea creatures, and Wrinkle Face and Iguana are protagonists of Phase IV and V fine-line scenes such as the Bean and Stick Ceremony (Donnan and McClelland 1999: 114-115), Ceremonial Badminton (Kutscher 1958), and the Burial Theme (Donnan and McClelland 1979). Although the meaning of such scenes is poorly understood, the frequent appearance of Wrinkle Face and Iguana indicates that they were central figures in Late Moche artwork and religion in both the northern and southern Moche regions.

Several Moche deities possess fangs and serpent belts. Quilter (2010: 62) suggests that although they are distinct entities, fanged deities may be considered as part of a "principal god complex." In a number of ways, Moche religion is a continuation of earlier Andean traditions (Cordy-Collins 1992; Quilter 2001), and Moche deities likely inherited fangs and serpent belts from supernatural beings of the Early Horizon Chavín and Cupisnique traditions (Benson 1972: 15, 27, 1975: 105, 1997a: 45, 2012: 61; Kutscher 1967: 122). Benson (1972: 27, 2012: 70) believes that Wrinkle Face is mountain deity, a likely suggestion given his frequent appearance in mountain scenes. Although Cupisnique was a coastal tradition (also referred to as Coastal Chavín), the Moche may have associated deities with fangs and serpent belts with the highland Chavín religious tradition (figure 1.6). As the primary source of fresh water, mountains are a focal point of religious practices in the Andes and they are often associated with important ancestral figures that control agricultural productivity. In contemporary ethnographic accounts, sacred mountains are anthropomorphic and can be conceptualized as having parts analogous to those of the human body (see Bastien 1995: 356-359). Serpents can represent flowing water in Andean art and thought (Smith 2012: 10-14), and the undulating serpent hair and belts of Chavín deities evoke rivers flowing from an ancestral mountain-being. As in other parts of the Andes, mountain (*apu*) veneration was a probable basis of Moche religion, as fresh water from the mountains was crucial for survival on the arid coast. By associating fanged deities with mountains, the Moche were actively continuing earlier traditions, and in doing so, they likely added a sense of legitimacy and an aura of timelessness to their practices and religious tenets.

Figure 4.1. Jar with low-relief copulation scene. Museo Larco, Lima. ML004365.

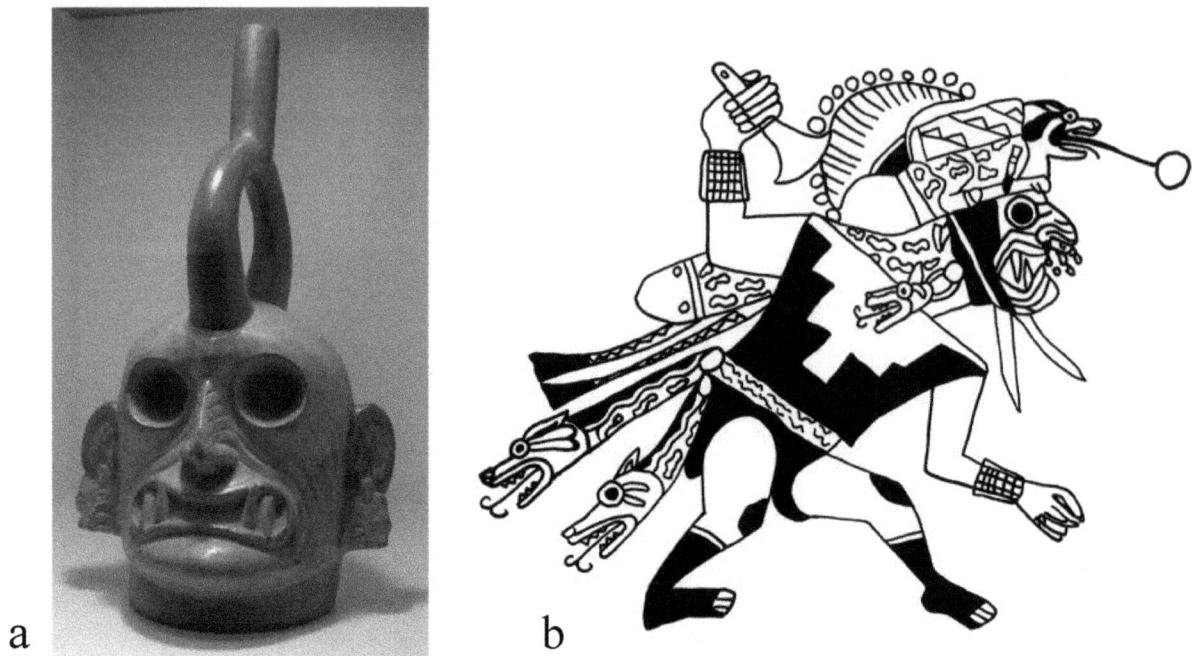

a

b

Figure 4.2. Representations of Wrinkle Face: a) Stirrup-spout vessel, Museo Larco; b) Wrinkle Face from fineline florero. Museo Larco, Lima. ML018882.

Figure 4.3. Jar with low-relief copulation scene (detail). Museo Larco, Lima. ML004365.

Figure 4.4. Stirrup-spout vessel in the form of Iguana. Museo Larco, Lima.

Wrinkle Face's frequent accomplice, Iguana, stands with hands clasped in back of the structure in which the pair copulates (figure 3.3). He is accompanied by a quadruped mammal that is likely a dog, based on other representations in which it appears with Wrinkle Face and Iguana. Interestingly, the dog is the only animal in the scene that is never anthropomorphized or depicted with apparent supernatural traits. Iguana is readily identifiable by his reptilian face, a sash over his shoulder or waist, a bird headdress, and almond-shaped eyes. He occasionally sports a serrated tail (Donnan and McClelland 1979: 6), and a long forked tongue protrudes from his mouth. Benson (2012: 68) suggests that Iguana is based on the species *Iguana iguana*, and Bourget (2006: 164) attributes Iguana to *Conolophus subcristanus*, a semi-aquatic coastal iguana, but precise identification is difficult, and Iguana is likely a generalized or composite reptile based one or more species.[8] Iguana's hands are commonly depicted as clasped, and while this would denote prayer, supplication, or humility in Western traditions, it is problematic to speculate its meaning in Moche art without additional evidence,

as meanings of hand gestures are not universal across cultures.

Iguana frequently appears alone as a three-dimensional deck figure on vessels (figure 3.4), but is usually paired with Wrinkle Face in several different painted and low-relief scenes, and the precise nature of the relationship between the two characters is unknown. The only known large-scale depiction of Iguana is a mural at Pañamarca (see Schaedel 1967: fig. 12; Trever, *et al.* 2013: 106-107, figs. 5 & 7), the southernmost monumental Moche site. The badly damaged mural places a solitary Iguana in opposition to the Strombus Monster, a creature that appears in Burial Theme scenes along with Wrinkle Face and Iguana, and in scenes in which Wrinkle Face and Iguana battle sea monsters. Recent excavations at Pañamarca by Trever and colleagues have also revealed additional mural depictions of Wrinkle Face engaged in combat with supernatural beings (Trever 2013). Benson (1975: 138) believes that Iguana is a death priest or Wrinkle Face's psychopomp. Berezkin (1980: 15) suggests that Wrinkle Face and Iguana are twins, as is often the case with mythical protagonists in ancient American traditions. It is noteworthy that in figure 4.4, Iguana's face has long striations similar to those of Wrinkle Face. A Phase II vessel portrays Wrinkle Face holding a crescent-shaped *tumi* knife and the severed head of Iguana, while standing over his decapitated body (Benson 1975: 140). Although the exact relationship between the two characters remains unclear, it was undoubtedly complex.

Since the late-1980s discovery of tombs in Sipán, in which Moche elites were found decked in garb similar to that worn by deities in Moche imagery, and several other excavations since that have yielded similar finds, scholars have eagerly interpreted Moche scenes as depictions of rulers or priests acting as deity impersonators in ritual. For example, a scene formerly known as the Presentation Theme (figure 1.7; see Donnan 1977), in which the blood of captives is collected in goblets and presented by a female and an anthropomorphic owl to a rayed being, was renamed the Sacrifice Ceremony, and the woman, owl, and rayed being were dubbed the Priestess, Owl Priest, and Warrior Priest (Quilter 2002: 165).[9] However, several scholars viewed Wrinkle Face's copulation scenes as portrayals of ritual prior to the Sipán discoveries. According to Larco Hoyle (1965: 101) the scenes

---

[8] *Conolophus subcristanus* is a marine iguana native only to the Galapagos Islands, and this attribution is unlikely, given that the Galapagos Islands are located in open sea more than 700 miles from the North Coast of Peru and there is no evidence of Moche visitation.

[9] Wrinkle Face and Iguana are notably absent from Presentation Theme/Sacrifice Ceremony scenes.

Figure 4.5. Rollout drawing of copulation scene on low-relief vessel.
Museo Nacional de Historia Natural, Santiago de Chile. After Donnan 1976: fig. 1.

have a ritual character. In Carrión Cachot's view (1959), the scenes combine mythological events and human ritualistic acts. She notes that deities are represented in the scenes, but the inclusion of severed body parts in one example (figure 3.5) suggests to her an accompanying act of female sacrifice (1959: 18). Noting the presence of body parts, Donnan (1976: 6) refers to the same as "a ceremony apparently involving sexual intercourse and human cannibalism." Donnan substantiates the claim of cannibalism by two figures in the scene that hold their hands to their mouths as if eating. Hocquenghem (cited in Bourget 2006: 158) views Wrinkle Face copulation scenes as part of mourning rituals.

Other scholars favor interpretation of Wrinkle Face copulation scenes as mythical narrative scenes. Benson (1972: 44) believes that the Wrinkle Face copulation scenes are mythological, and adds that they could represent the origin of the Moche people (1997a: 45, 2012: 69). Although Hocquenghem and Golte (Hocquenghem 1989; Hocquenghem and Golte 1987) suggest that the myths represented were reenacted as part of the Andean ritual calendar, they relate the scenes to myths recorded in the Colonial-period Huarochirí Manuscript (1991). Bourget (2006: 160-167) adopts an inverse approach, and in his view, Wrinkle Face copulation scenes are primarily narrative representations of ritual events with possible mythical components. Quilter (1997: 121, 2002: 165-166) notes that as myth is portrayed or evoked in ritual, Moche elites dressing as deities and visual representations of deities in Moche artwork both drew content and ideology from the same source: Moche myth. Given the relationship between myth and ritual, and the presence of supernatural elements such as flying anthropomorphic birds, I approach Wrinkle Face copulation scenes as mythical in nature, and assume that the scenes were understood as narratives.

While it is possible that costumed priests could have ceremonially reenacted mythical events involving Wrinkle Face and Iguana, no definitive archaeological evidence of human impersonation of the pair has yet been found.[10] Furthermore, the presence of the duo in various other types of scenes suggests that the copulation scenes are fragments of a larger mythical narrative, or an episode in a series of stories in which Wrinkle Face and Iguana are protagonists.

As in most other examples in which Wrinkle Face copulates within a structure, the Larco Jar portrays a scene to the left of the sex act in which birds prepare a liquid (figure 3.6). A larger bird descends a set of steps and pours the liquid onto the back of Wrinkle Face as he copulates. Behind Iguana, on the other side of the structure, another building contains two human figures that appear to hold staffs and a bird hovers above them inside of the structure, while another bird stands in front of it (figure 3.7). The figures are identifiable as women based on the skirts they wear and their cropped, shoulder-length hair. Men typically wear head-cloths or some other type of headdress in Moche art. Each of the women has one hand to her mouth. Donnan (1976: 6) interprets this gesture as eating, and Larco Hoyle (1965: 101) views raised hands as an attitude of prayer. Although it is difficult to determine the meaning of such gestures, as in the case of Iguana's clenched hands, it is also possible that the hand-to-mouth gesture indicates verbal communication, as the bird facing the structure also makes the same gesture toward the figures inside.

---

[10] However, Bourget (2006: 26-32) raises the possibility that the main burial in the Warrior-Priest tomb at Huaca de la Cruz may have been an impersonator of Wrinkle Face, based on associated accoutrements and ceramics, and that a child accompanying the main burial may have represented Iguana.

Figure 4.6. Jar with low-relief copulation scene. Museo Larco, Lima. ML004365.

Figure 4.7. Jar with low-relief copulation scene. Museo Larco, Lima. ML004365.

Figure 4.8. Spout-and-handle vessel with low-relief copulation scene.
Museo Larco, Lima. ML004360.

The significance of the second structure and the women and birds in and around it is unclear. Benson (2012: 69) suggests that the two women in the structure may accompany the woman coupled with Wrinkle Face in her burial after she dies, linking the scene to widespread origin myths in the Americas in which a woman is killed after mating with a jaguar, although it is not apparent that the woman copulating with Wrinkle Face will be killed afterwards. Other authors speculate that the women in the structure are awaiting their turn to copulate with the deity (Hocquenghem and Golte 1987: 278; Kauffmann-Doig 1979: 59; Larco Hoyle 1965: 101), but these authors posit a ritualistic element into the scene that may not be present. Another possibility is that the birds are detaining the figures inside, as the larger bird outside of the structure would bar their exit.

In one example of the scene (figure 3.8), only the dog and the structure that houses Wrinkle Face and the woman with whom he copulates are portrayed. The same scene is repeated on both sides of the vessel. The lack of the additional structure and characters suggests that Wrinkle Face's copulation is the most significant portion of the scene. This is likely an example of "key scenario redundancy," in which the most essential elements of a narrative are repeated more often than those of lesser significance (Quilter 1997: 116). In other words, the copulation of Wrinkle Face and the woman is the focus and pivotal point of the narrative, and although other elements and characters add content, they are ultimately inessential details that are not necessary for evoking the story to viewers who are familiar with the entirety of the narrative.[11]

Although most authors place the steps and the mixing scene as the beginning of the sequence (assuming a left to right reading order) in rollout drawings, for the example found in Plaza 1 of Huaca de la Luna, Bourget favors placement of the house with two human figures inside at the beginning of the narrative, rather than the end (figure 3.9a; Bourget 2006: 157). In Bourget's interpretation of the scene as a multipart human-enacted ritual (2006: 164-167), the first scene in the sequence is the house with two female occupants, in which the women give the stick to a bird, which it

uses to prepare the liquid in the second scene.[12] In the third scene in Bourget's sequence, a bird takes the prepared liquid down the steps to a ceremonial precinct, and in the climactic final scene, the bird pours the liquid on the pair as they copulate. In comparing Bourget's arrangement of the scene to the Larco Jar, Iguana and the bird that is placed between his back and the second structure have been separated in the drawing, and the feathers of Iguana's headdress no longer touch the roof, creating additional negative space at either end of the drawing that is not present or implied on the actual vessel. Figure 3.9b gives a more natural division at the column of negative space between the back of the second structure and the birds preparing the mixture. Furthermore, Bourget's illustration downplays the symmetrical and repetitive quadripartite composition of the scene as it wraps around the vessel, with an alternating pattern of a cluster of "outdoor" figures and a structure, followed by another cluster of "outdoor" figures and another structure. A symmetrical composition in the scene may present oppositional pairings of indoor and outdoor, and is consistent with a general bipartite or quadripartite compositional trend in the decoration of other Moche globular vessels.

If the vessel does in fact portray sequential events, the placement of the separation of the scene is crucial because it affects the entire reading of the image. However, Golte (2009: 27-52) notes that the rollout drawings that are more legible to scholars who are accustomed to reading imagery on a flat plane are misleading, as globular Moche vessels were meant to be experienced by being held and rotated in the hands. It is unlikely that the strict linearity of the rollout drawing reflects the intent of Moche artists. Illustrators presuppose a certain reading order at the outset of creating a rollout drawing, and in doing so, whether deliberate or not, favor and encourage certain interpretations while discouraging others. Furthermore, in flattening the image, illustrators often compress, distort, or omit details, and change spatial relationships (Golte 2009: 27-52). As it does not seem that any one character appears multiple times within the scene on the Larco Jar, with the possible exception of the birds, it may be that the image shows events that are

---

[11] It is also possible that the other half of the mold was lost or destroyed, causing the artist to repeat the scene from the same half of the mold in order to complete the vessel. In either case, the fact that the vessel was produced with the same scene on both sides suggests that the narrative retained its essence without the additional building and other characters.

[12] It is not clear that the sticks held by the women inside the structure are the same as the stick used by the bird to prepare the liquid. The women's sticks appear to be larger and shaped differently, and I interpret them as agricultural implements.

Figure 4.9. Rollout drawings of copulation scene on low-relief jar from Huaca de la Luna, Plaza 1: a) with placement of the structure containing women at the left of the scene. After drawing by Jorge Sachún; b) with placement of the structure containing women at the right of the scene. Drawn by author and Eric Heller after drawing by Jorge Sachún.

Figure 4.10. Examples of the fisher headdress: a) Jar with low-relief copulation scene (detail). Museo Larco, Lima. ML004365; b) Fine-line boat scene (detail). After drawing by Donna McClelland; c) Fine-line sea lion hunting scene (detail). After drawing by Donna McClelland.

occuring simultaneously with no discernible beginning or end in the narrative. In such a case, whether the second structure was in a position to the right or to the left of the other elements in the image may ultimately have had little bearing on the meaning of the scene to the ancient viewer, who would not have experienced the scene linearly with a clearly demarcated beginning and end.

A band of waves serves as the lower border below the scene on the Larco Jar and other examples of the Wrinkle Face copulation scene. The waves indicate that the events may take place in or near the sea (Benson 1975: 110). DeMott (cited in Benson 1975: 110) notes that the birds in Wrinkle Face copulation scenes wear "fisher" headdresses, which are headbands or diadems with two vertical strips projecting from the front (figure 3.10). Wrinkle Face wears the headdress as he battles sea monsters and pilots a raft in boat scenes (figure 3.10b), and it is clearly associated with the coast and maritime activities. In Moche seal-hunting scenes, hunters also wear the fisher headdress (figure 3.10c), and in two other examples of the Wrinkle Face house copulation scene, human figures wearing fisher headdresses replace some of the birds in the scene

(figure 3.5).[13] On the Larco Jar, only the bird that descends the steps and pours the liquid onto the copulating pair wears the fisher headdress, however this example differs slightly from other known examples because there is a smaller head, perhaps that of a bird, projecting from the front.[14]

Guano islands were of great significance to the Moche, and the birds represented on the Larco Jar may be identifiable as species that frequent them. There is a group of guano islands off the northern

[13] In a similar substitution, in one example of the Burial Theme, Wrinkle Face and Iguana are replaced by anthropomorphized birds that lower the casket into the burial chamber (Donnan and McClelland 1979: 6). The mortuary association between Wrinkle Face and birds may also be illustrated in examples of scenes in which Wrinkle Face is being led by cormorants to what Benson (1975: 110-111) believes is the underworld on the other side of the sea. A well-known vessel that portrays an owl-headed curer and a recumbent Wrinkle Face beneath a blanket (see Quilter 2010: 130-131) is another instance of a curious interaction between Wrinkle Face and a bird with possible mortuary connotations, and may be a related scene. In other examples, Wrinkle Face rides on the back of a bird.

[14] The smaller head projecting from the bird's fisher headdress does not appear on the otherwise similar rollout drawing of the example excavated in Plaza 1 of Huaca de la Luna. It is not clear if this detail was omitted or overlooked in the preparation of the drawing, as it is subtle, or if it is not present in the actual vessel.

North Coast, one off the southern North Coast, and an island chain off of the Central and South Coasts (Benson 1995: 245). Based on sculptures and other objects found in guano deposits, it is apparent that the Moche revered guano islands by making pilgrimages and leaving offerings (Benson 1972: 78, 1995; Kubler 1985). Moche artifacts have been found as far south as the Chincha Islands, off of Peru's South Coast (Benson 1995: 253). Larco Hoyle (1946: 163; also Benson 1972: 78, 1995: 250) suggests that the Moche may have ben interested in guano for its use as a potent crop fertilizer. The Guanay Cormorant (*Phalocrocorax bougainvillii*), the Peruvian Booby (*Sula variegata*), and the Peruvian Pelican (*Pelecanus thagus*) are the primary guano producing birds on the islands off of the coast of Peru (Benson 1995: 246-247; Rostworowski de Diez Canseco 1997: 34), where they nest in large numbers in relative safety. The general lack of rainfall near the coast allows guano deposits that would otherwise be washed away to reach significant depths.

Larco Hoyle (1965: 101) identified the birds in Wrinkle Face copulation scenes as cormorants, but there are at least two different types of bird represented on the Larco Jar, one of which is identifiable as the Peruvian Booby. The bird that is mixing and the bird above it, as well as the bird in front of the structure that houses the women are likely of the same type, as they all have similarly shaped wings without delineated feathers, a gently curved beak, and an incision that begins at the back of the eye and terminates at the top of the throat. Although the Larco Jar lacks pigment, save for white slip in the recesses to make the elements in higher relief stand out in sharper contrast, the incision that delineates the beak is likely a distinctive feature of the Peruvian Booby. On the low-relief vessel, the incised line could be read as a separation of two fields of color. Peruvian Boobies are white, except for a black "facemask" around the eyes and grayish beak. The smaller bird that is within the structure with the women is likely the same type, but it is small and lacks fine detail.

A unique Moche IV vessel (figure 3.11) has the head of a bird, and the body of the vessel is white, with the exception of a chevron pattern around the spout, a red spot on the "rump," and a red-slip "facemask" around the eye and slightly curved beak that make it identifiable as a Peruvian Booby.[15] The beak shape and facial markings are strongly

---

[15] Although black pigment was used on some Moche vessels, Moche IV painters typically favored the use of red and white slip.

reminiscent of the examples on the Larco Jar. While Benson (1997b) tentatively identifies the bird as a cormorant, she posits that the odd shape of the vessel and white pigment make a visual pun between guano bird and guano island. The red chevron band around the spout of the bird vessel represents a rope, and suggests that it may be an offering, perhaps destined for a guano island. A rope, whether around the neck of a vessel or the neck of a victim may mark it as a sacrifice (Benson 1975: 108; Donnan 1996: 146-147), and among Moche wooden objects found in guano island deposits, most represent seated captives with similar ropes around their necks. Furthermore, vessels that may contain sacrificial blood and are tied with ropes around their necks are often portrayed in boat scenes (Quilter 1997: 128). Wrinkle Face sometimes pilots a boat laden with similarly tied jars or captives, and it is possible that his destination is a guano island, suggesting an additional link between Wrinkle Face, guano islands, and guano-producing birds.

Figure 4.11. Vessel in the form of a bird.
Museo Larco, Lima. ML010478.
After Benson 1997b: 115.

The larger anthropomorphic bird that pours the liquid and wears the fisher headdress differs from the others, having a hooked beak, wings in which the feathers are clearly defined, a prominent "chin," and an ear resembling that of a human. While it is possible that the bird's chin represents a pelican's gular pouch, or even the white spot that is found on the upper throat of the Guanay Cormorant, anthropomorphized birds such as owls, hummingbirds, and Muscovy Ducks often have prominent chins in Moche art. Furthermore, the recurved beak of the bird with the fisher headdress does not resemble the beaks of the Peruvian Pelican or the Guanay Cormorant, which are straight, except for a sharp hook at the tip. The larger size, more elaborate dress, and more humanlike features of the bird with the fisher headdress likely denote greater importance in relation to the other birds, and it may represent a deity. During the early Colonial period, fishermen revered a guano god referred to as Guamancanfac or Guamancantac, and as Rostworowski de Diez Canseco (1997: 34-35) notes, *guamán* is the Quechua term for a bird of prey, and the suffix -canfac or -cantac is likely of Muchic origin. The blended name of this deity may suggest Inca syncretism with preexisting local beliefs, although there were coastal variants of Quechua prior to Inca domination (Quilter, *et al.* 2010: 361). The Osprey (*Pandion haliaetus*), a fish-eating bird of prey that commonly appears in Moche art, should not be ruled out as a possible prototype, and the bird that pours liquid on Wrinkle Face's back may indeed be a Moche guano god.

The bird that mixes the liquid does so over a fire, as denoted by the hearthstones or tripod legs beneath the vessel (figs. 3.6 & 3.9; Larco Hoyle 1965: 101). Benson (1975: 110) observes that this episode likely represents the preparation of *chicha*, the fermented beverage made from corn. Moore (1989: 686; see also Shimada 1994: 221-222) argues that although there are a variety of methods of *chicha* production, all involve the basic steps of maize preparation (which includes the conversion of starches into sugars by germinating the maize or by mixing saliva with maize flour), cooking the prepared maize in water, and fermentation. Among the Moche, *chicha* production was likely a ceremonialized act (Donnan 1976: 131).[16]

In the next sequence of the scene, the prepared liquid is transported down the steps by a bird

wearing a fisher headdress. The vessel from which the bird pours the liquid may be self-referential for the Larco Jar, hinting at an intended use. Arboleda (1981: 103) believes that the bird administers the liquid to Wrinkle Face in the form of an enema, but other scholars agree that the liquid is being poured onto Wrinkle Face's back or the genitals of the copulating pair (Benson 1972: 144, 1975: 110; Kauffmann-Doig 1979: 59; Larco Hoyle 1965: 101). In Bourget's interpretation of the scene as a ritual, he reads the steps as the entrance to a ceremonial precinct. There is probably some conceptual overlap with Moche monumental architecture, but the steps also likely represent a stylized mountain (Benson 1975: 119).

As the primary sources of fresh water, mountains are symbolically charged and of paramount importance throughout the Andes. Moche ceramic representations suggest that mountains may have been the setting for sacrifices to ensure the flow of water (Benson 1972: 34; Hocquenghem 1989: 183; Zighelboim 1995). Typically in mountain sacrifice scenes such as the example illustrated in figure 3.12, a prone human figure is slumped over a central peak, and a series of other figures are situated on and around the mountains. Another figure lays below (or perhaps the same figure – see Zighelboim 1995), and in other examples, a stream of red slip connects the figure on the peak to a nude figure who has apparently been cast down from the mountain or washed down in the stream that flows from beneath the upper figure's hair. The sacrifice of victims and flow of blood may invoke and perpetuate the flow of water. In some examples, Wrinkle Face and Iguana are among the onlookers or overseers, suggesting that they are associated with mountain sacrifice (figure 3.13).

Moche artists apparently portrayed mountains in a number of ways. Although there are others with fewer or more peaks, most Moche representations of mountains have five peaks, reminiscent of a human hand (Donnan 1976: 108; Tello 1938: 254). In some instances, a stepped wave with a prone human on the crest and another figure lying on the bottom step that is presumably dead, similar to examples of mountain sacrifice scenes, is flanked by Wrinkle Face and Iguana (3.14a). The stepped wave scene may be an abstracted version of the mountain sacrifice scene (Bock 2003: 312-313), suggesting that the stepped form on the Larco Jar may also represent a mountain. A recently discovered step-shaped Moche carved stone altar on top of Cerro Campana (Franco Jordán 2012: 303-306), located between Huacas de Moche and Huaca

---

[16] A Moche vessel in the Museo Bruning in Lambayeque portrays two modeled figures making *chicha* (Donnan 1976: plate 5). Bourget (2006: 160) believes that the *chicha*-mixing scene in the Bruning is a more elaborate version of the birds making the liquid in the copulation scene. Indeed the scenes are similar and a vessel on hearthstones or tripod legs and stick for mixing are represented on both vessels, but the human figures on the Museo Bruning vessel display no obvious supernatural attributes, and therefore suggest no direct relation to the mixing episode undertaken by birds in the copulation scenes.

Figure 4.12. Stirrup-spout vessel with mountain scene. Museo Larco, Lima.

Figure 4.13. Blackware stirrup-spout vessel with mountain scene. De Young Fine Arts Museum, San Francisco.

a

b

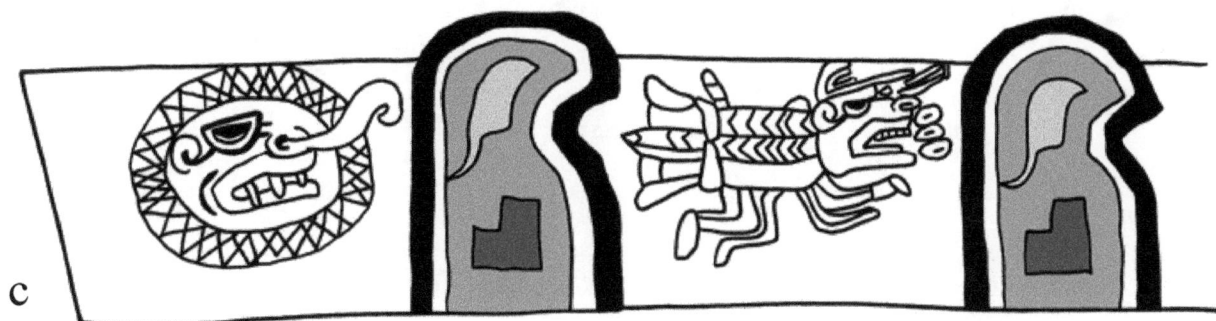

c

Figure 4.14. Examples of stepped forms: a) Stirrup-spout vessel in the form of a stepped wave. Museo de la Nación, Lima; b) Moche stone altar, Cerro Campana, Peru. After Franco Jordan 2012: fig. 11; c) Frieze from Garagay showing stepped waves. After Quilter 2001: fig. 3.

Figure 4.15. Vessel with sacrifice scene. After Berezkin 1980: fig. 5b.

Figure 4.16. Examples of the half fist gesture: a) Carved and incised bone spatula handle. After Donnan 1976 :fig. 102; b) Jar with phallic spout. After Larco 1965: 37; c) Fine-line vessel portraying warriors (detail). After drawing by Donna McClelland.

Cao Viejo (figure 3.14b), is nearly identical in shape to the stepped form on the Larco Jar. Similar stepped altars have been found on the upper terrace of the Early Intermediate period Central Coast site of Huaca Pucllana (Quilter pers. comm. 2013), and earlier examples from a building on the summit of a pyramid at the Central Coast site of Cardal date back to the Initial period (Burger and Salazar-Burger 1991: 281, fig. 3; Quilter 2001: 24). In artwork, an Initial Period precursor to the Moche stepped wave may be found on the atrium frieze at the Central Coast site of Garagay (Quilter pers. comm. 2013). In the frieze, designs consisting of two steps surmounted by a curved form punctuate images of supernatural creatures (3.14c).

The stepped pattern on Wrinkle Face's tunic may also refer to mountains, alluding to his probable identity as a mountain deity. When rendered in fine-line, the design on his tunic resembles two opposed stepped forms in red slip (figure 3.2b). On some vessels that portray mountain sacrifice, Wrinkle Face and Iguana flank a curved mountain, but two opposed stepped forms are placed at the base of the mountain, which includes a sacrificial victim on the summit (or summits, as in the example illustrated in figure 3.15). In some instances, the opposed stepped forms surmount a frontally rendered set of three steps, suggesting that the stepped forms may represent a series of stylized mountains. The opposed stepped forms on mountain sacrifice scenes immediately recall the typical pattern on Wrinkle

Face's tunic. If this stylized depiction of mountains is analogous to Wrinkle Face's tunic, his head may represent a central, craggy (as suggested by his wrinkles) mountain peak. The step-shaped altar on top of Cerro Campana and the association of the stepped form with scenes of mountain sacrifice strongly imply that the bird with the fisher headdress on the Larco Jar descends a stylized mountain (which also resembles a stepped altar) bearing a jar of liquid.

A specific hand gesture represented in Moche art adds another conceptual layer to mountain symbolism. The "half fist" gesture is made by holding the fist aloft with the middle knuckle slightly elevated, and the gesture is made by male figures in Moche ceramics. Hands making the gesture are occasionally produced as solitary objects in a variety of media (figure 3.16a). Donnan (1976: 112, 1996: 137) relates the half fist gesture to mountains, as their representations share distinct formal similarities in Moche art. Bourget (2006: 123) cites an example in which the half fist gesture is made by the principal figure in a mountain sacrifice scene, and he believes that the half fist carries phallic connotations (see also Zighelboim 1995: 170). In some figural anthropomorphic vessels in which the spout is an erect penis, the figure makes the half fist gesture (figure 3.16b). The occasional substitution of the head of a war club with a half fist in warrior scenes (figure 3.16c) also suggests that the half fist is a symbol of masculinity, and perhaps lends phallic connotations to the war club.

In contemporary and ethnohistoric accounts, the Andean landscape is gendered, and the Moche likely espoused similar beliefs. The earth is typically considered to be a feminine entity, and mountains are masculine, as expressed in the Inca concept of the bipartite social and cosmological organizing principal of *hanan* (associated with masculine, right, and upper) and *hurin* (associated with feminine, left, and lower).[17] While mountains are generally male, irrigable valleys are female (Salomon 1991: 15). These gendered oppositions are relative to context and are not fixed, as they are in the Western Cartesian tradition (Dean 2007: 506); for example, water is generally feminine, but masculine when equated to semen as it fertilizes the earth (Classen 1993: 13). In this anthropomorphic view of the cosmos, the bilateral symmetry of the human body has dualistic analogs in landscape, and the principals that govern human social organization and behavior are also inherent in natural phenomena.

In some Moche examples, an erect penis forms the central peak in a vessel that represents mountains (figure 3.17; Benson 1972: 146; Bergh 1993: 80), which strongly suggests that, like that of the Inca, the Moche landscape was gendered and anthropomorphic. To extend the metaphor, river water from a phallic mountain that fertilizes the river valley below could be analogous to semen, suggesting a gendered mountain/earth dichotomy in Moche belief. Interestingly, the association of phalli with mountains is echoed in a passage in the early Colonial Huarochirí Manuscript (1991: 78), which describes a huaca called Rucana Coto ("finger-shaped mountain") who was known to have a large penis, and to whom men would pray to have their members enlarged. It is noteworthy that the symbolic association between fingers, phalli, and mountains in the Huarochirí Manuscript is also present in the Moche symbolic vocabulary through the half fist gesture and ceramic mountain scene vessels, suggesting that some of the themes regarding the anthropomorphic and gendered landscape have considerable temporal and cross-cultural continuity. The Larco Jar incorporates this symbolism by associating a mountain deity with sexual fertility.

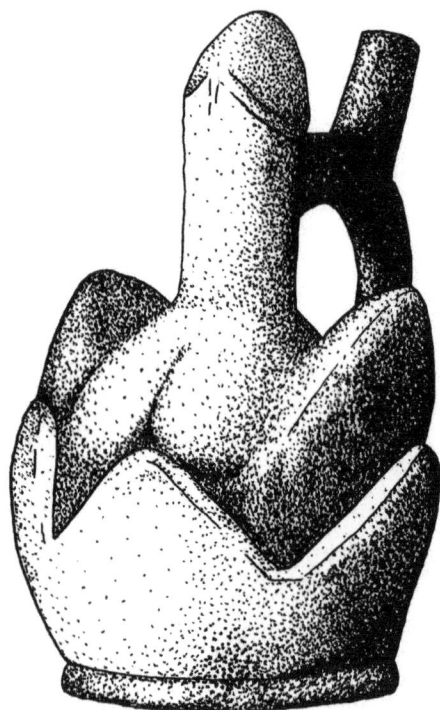

Figure 4.17. Stirrup-spout vessel with phallic mountain. After Bourget 2006: fig. 2.78.

Figure 4.18. Jar with low-relief copulation scene (detail). Museo Larco, Lima. ML004365.

On the Larco Jar and other similar examples, a stirrup-spout vessel is placed near the heads of Wrinkle Face and the woman with whom he

---

[17] For the Inca, gold (masculine) and silver (feminine) were also complementary pairs. The same was likely true for the Moche. For example, the tombs of Sipán reflect a similar bimetallic symbolic duality, with gold prevalently placed on the right of the deceased individuals, and silver on the left (Alva 2001: 225; Alva and Donnan 1993: 221-223).

copulates (figure 3.18). The placement of the vessel may suggest to the viewer that the structure has a wall upon which the jar is hung, rather than being open on the sides. However, the stirrup-spout vessel is a symbolically charged form in the Andes, and its deliberate placement near the couple likely conveys additional meaning in the scene. Scholars have raised the possibility that certain conventionalized objects in Moche depictions may be ideographic in nature, and may represent strides toward the development of a formalized writing system. Based on the frequent appearance of beans in association with figures who may have been messengers in Moche depictions, Larco Hoyle (1939: 85-124) suggested that Moche elites may have encrypted messages in different assortments of beans. Donnan and McClelland demonstrate the use of specific hand signs among Moche figures and short-hand geographic locators in scenes to signify different environments, and they note that such symbols appear more frequently in Phase IV imagery (1999: 292), and become more abstract in Phase V (1999: 294). Jackson (2002, 2008, 2011) argues that certain Moche iconographic conventions acquired logographic characteristics, and artists may have employed rebus in imagery. The severed heads and legs bound by ropes on one example (figure 3.5) of the copulation scene that led some scholars to believe that the scene represents a ritual with human sacrifice and cannibalism may not necessarily be part of the scene, but rather may add clarification or additional content to the image as ideographic symbols.

Depictions of stirrup-spout vessels and other vessel types appear with some frequency on Moche ceramics. Benson (1975: 109) notes that single depictions of stirrup-spout vessels are often associated with the most significant figure in the scene, usually a deity (Benson 1975: 109). Dancing death figure scenes include depictions of vessels such as *floreros* and spout-and-handle vessels that do not appear in dance scenes that involve human figures (Donnan 1982: 100). Benson (1975: 108) believes that the Moche associated the form of the stirrup-spout vessel with Chavín and Chavín mountain deities, and that the form itself carried symbolic value. As previously noted, Quilter (2010: 43) argues that the stirrup spout may convey *tinkuy*, a highly significant and symbolically charged conjoining of two streams of liquid or other opposed forces, when poured. The act of sexual intercourse may also be considered a form of *tinkuy* (Harrison 1989: 30). The placement of stirrup-spout vessels near the heads of Wrinkle Face and the woman with whom he couples may likewise emphasize the sexual act, or denote it as a *tinkuy* convergence.

In the known mythic traditions in the Andes, as important beings transform into huacas, they are often lithified and become associated with mountains. Several of Wrinkle Face's traits suggest a relationship with mountains, such as his resemblance to the deities of the highland Chavín tradition, the stepped pattern on his tunic, and the serpents that hang from his belt, resembling flowing rivers. On the arid coast, which receives little rainfall, fresh water from mountain streams and rivers makes cultivation possible. Wrinkle Face and Iguana are portrayed in association with mountain sacrifice scenes, the likely objective of which was to invoke the flow of water. As in ethnographic and ethnohistoric sources, the Moche landscape may have been animate and gendered, with masculine mountains and feminine irrigable valleys. The setting of the scene on the Larco Jar is the coast, as suggested by the presence of birds associated with the sea and guano islands, and a border of waves beneath the scene. In this instance, as a mountain deity, Wrinkle Face may metaphorically illustrate the fructifying effects of mountain streams on the lowlands, and portray mythical tales that trace the origin and arrival of irrigation to the otherwise parched coast.

The spatial and complementary relationship between the coast and the mountains may be made apparent on the Larco Jar. The identity of the woman with whom Wrinkle Face copulates is unclear, and lacking clothing, facial markings, and accouterments, it cannot be ascertained whether or not she is a deity or human. However, in formal terms, the woman is lying flat on her back like the earth, while Wrinkle Face is above her, with his back sloped like a mountain, which could simultaneously convey a cosmological relationship between male and female as well as the origins of the two respective characters. The meeting point of the mountains and the coast may also represent a convergence that conveys the concept of *tinkuy* (Harrison 1989: 103).

Sex and crop fertilization by water are closely linked in Andean belief systems. In the Huarochirí Manuscript (1991), storm water and downward-flowing water are masculine, and storms and flashfloods are likened to male warfare (Salomon 1991: 15). Bergh (1993: 82-83) notes instances in which foamy or fast-moving water is conceptualized as semen from a mountain god that fertilizes Pachamama, the female earth deity. In

Chuschi, in the department of Ayacucho, irrigation water is equated to the semen of the Wamanis, mountain deities and keepers of animals who are in charge of water (Isbell 1978: 143). According to Salomon, "The hydraulic embrace of moving water and enduring earth was imagined as sex" (1991: 15). In an episode in the Huarochirí Manuscript (1991), the deity Cuni Raya pursues Caui Llaca and the baby that he sired from Anchicocha in the highlands to the islands off the coast near Pachacamac, which follows the course of the Lurín River from its headwaters to the sea, suggesting the myth alludes the fructifying effect of the river on the valley (Huarochirí Manuscript 1991: 48, footnote 53).[18] Drought or flooding are also frequent punishments for sexual transgressions in sources in coastal and highland traditions (Bergh 1993: 83), revealing the delicate equilibrium that must be maintained in order to keep the Andean cosmos in balance, and demonstrating that human actions that counter social order threaten the order of natural phenomena. In the gendered anthropomorphic landscape of the Andes, human sexual intercourse is a microcosmic event that mirrors the large-scale processes of crop irrigation and the circulation of fluids between the mountains and the coast.

Intercourse between deities or ancestral figures and the advent and cleaning of irrigation systems are also closely linked in myth and contemporary beliefs. In Huarochirí, during the September canal-cleaning ceremonies, an impersonator of the ancestor Huari descends the length of the canal while a young woman waits for him in the cultivated fields (Dumézil and Duviols cited in Hocquenghem 1989: 59). During the festival of Yarqa Aspiy in Chuschi, the cleaning and repair of the canals and the flow of water to the fields represent the sexual union of the mountain huaca Wamani and Mama Pacha, and her subsequent impregnation (Isbell 1978: 138-144). In the Huarochirí Manuscript (1991: 62-63), Paria Caca creates an irrigation system in exchange for sleeping with the beautiful Chuqui Suso. Pumas, foxes, snakes, and birds help him clean and fix the canal that he makes for her. Paria Caca and Chuqui Suso sleep together, then she goes to the mouth of a canal and turns to stone, or in other words, becomes a huaca.[19] Wrinkle Face appears to play a similar role to Wamani, Paria Caca, and Cuni Raya, as a mountain huaca who sleeps with a coastal woman, and metaphorically brings fructifying irrigation water to the coast.[20]

The Moche provided water to their crops through an extensive system of canals, and even linked the irrigation systems of the Moche and Chicama valleys (Benson 1972: 85; see Quilter 2002: 157-158), and as previously noted, human actors who donned divine costumes at the huacas likely exerted will to control the flow of water from the mountains to the coastal valleys. In the Huarochirí Manuscript (1991), Cuni Raya Viracocha is given credit for making the villages, fields, terraces, and irrigation canals. Wrinkle Face may have held similar status in Moche belief, as a mountain deity associated with the flow of water to the coast. His serpent belt hangs from his body as he copulates, reminiscent of a river flowing from a mountain. He also shares another characteristic with the aforementioned huacas in that, based on his zoomorphic retinue consisting of Iguana, sea birds, and the dog, he is ostensibly a keeper or master of animals. If the Moche myth depicted on the vessel follows a structure similar to Early Colonial versions, the two women holding digging sticks in the other structure could be outraged family members who are detained by the birds while Wrinkle Face dallies, or perhaps they are drought-ridden farmers who call for water, and Wrinkle Face has intercourse with a woman in exchange (and as a metaphorical substitution) for bringing irrigation and fertility to their crops.

The concoction prepared and poured by the birds on the Larco Jar also relates to sex and fertility (Larco Hoyle 1965: 101). The transport of liquid by the birds down the stepped form refers to the movement of fertilizing water down the mountains to the

---

[18] Salomon (1991: 10) describes Cuni Raya as a "trickster-demiurge embodying the transformation of landforms by water." Hocquenghem and Golte (1987:2 81-293) relate Wrinkle Face's erotic scenes to passages in the Huarochirí Manuscript (1991), although relating myths recorded during the Colonial period to Moche imagery must be approached cautiously.

[19] In another instance, Anchi Cara and a beautiful woman named Huayllama argue over use of the water from a spring. The two have intercourse and turn into stone, and then some water comes from the spring. People pay homage to Anchi Cara when they clean the canal (Huarochirí Manuscript 1991: 134-135).

[20] While it would be hasty and speculative to claim that myths recorded in the Huarochirí Manuscript and in ethnographic accounts are identical to the myth portrayed on the Larco Jar, there are striking similarities. Overall structures of mythical narratives may endure, but caution must be exercised, given the regional, cultural, and social differences between the Moche and Colonial and present-day peoples. Mythical and religious beliefs may be resilient and conservative in nature, but I acknowledge that portions of myths may be added, emphasized, deemphasized, modified, or deleted to suit specific historically contingent ideologies or social circumstances. Ostensibly similar myths are most useful as analogies until continuity from recorded myths and histories to the Early Intermediate Period North Coast can be adequately demonstrated.

coastal valleys. Across the Americas, birds hold special significance for their ability to transcend upper and terrestrial cosmological realms through flight, which is a possible rationale for depicting birds as the agents of transportation of the liquid between elevations. The liquid is likely *chicha*, which is also related to semen in parts of the Andes through metaphor, and one type of *chicha* made on the North Coast is milky-white, similar in appearance to semen (Bergh 1993: 83-84).

Throughout the Americas, birds and fruit are also metaphorically associated with sexual intercourse (e.g. Chinchilla Mazariegos 2010). In an episode in the Huarochirí Manuscript (1991), the relationship between birds, sex, and fruit is explicit. Cuni Raya sees the beautiful virgin huaca Caui Llaca weaving beneath a lucuma tree, and he transforms into a bird, ejaculates onto a fruit that drops down beside her, and she becomes pregnant when she eats it. Later, when she discovers that it was Cuni Raya who impregnated her, she takes her son to the sea near Pachacamac, and they become rocky islands (Huarochirí Manuscript 1991: 46-48). Significantly, the islands just off the coast of Pachacamac that are associated with Caui Llaca and her son are guano islands. The appearance of birds associated with guano islands is also significant in the Larco Jar scene in this regard. Bird guano is thick and white, and may have been metaphorically linked to semen through its superficial resemblance, as appears to have been the case in the Cuni Raya myth. Furthermore, *chicha*, the liquid that was most likely contained in Moche vessels such as the Larco Jar, may also relate to bird guano via semen. The concoction prepared by the birds and subsequently poured onto Wrinkle Face emphasizes fertility or perhaps renders it a reproductive act.

Chicha is closely related to fertility and bodily fluids in Moche symbolism and that of other Andean cultures. As a final product of a successful harvest, *chicha* is in some regards the culmination of the agricultural cycle. A common method of *chicha* preparation in the Andes involves mixing maize flour with saliva, which aids in fermentation.[21] That the Moche viewed an analogy between *chicha* and semen is readily apparent in jars that take the form of ithyphallic male figures and were likely used to serve *chicha* or pour

libations (figure 3.16b). In known examples, regularly spaced perforations around the mouth of the jar would make effective pouring difficult, thus forcing the user to pour or drink directly from the phallus-shaped spout (Larco Hoyle 1965: 81), and equating the vessels' liquid contents to semen both through vessel form and performance. Middle-Horizon Wari face-neck jars that are decorated as rulers or important ancestors were used to dispense *chicha* at feasting events (Cook 2004: 157; Nash 2012: 90-91), suggesting that the Wari likened the *chicha* contained therein to human bodily fluids. Moche jar necks decorated with skulls, naturalistically rendered faces, or the faces of fanged beings, and the contents of these vessels may have been understood similarly. According to Bray (2000), the *urpu*, a large, distinctive imperial *chicha* vessel, represents an abstracted portrayal of the Inca ruler, essentializing the royal body to emblems of office such as large ear spools and elaborately decorated tunics. Bray's observations suggest that *chicha* may have been conceptualized as the liquid substance of the Inca body, intertwining notions of royalty and agricultural abundance. Arguably, Moche, Wari, and Inca sovereigns promulgated ideologies of rulership involving their ability to reward physical labor and loyalty through the transformation and redistribution of agricultural surplus, and they inserted these discourses into what were likely commonsense conceptions of the relationship of *chicha* to the vital fluids of the human body.

The imagery on the Larco Jar alludes to a probable metaphorical domain populated by fluids that are white and are associated with the body and human and agricultural fertility. Mountain runoff water, *chicha*, semen, guano, and perhaps saliva share these characteristics. Rivers can be viewed as vital, fertilizing fluids that flow from anthropomorphic mountains. Guano is a potent fertilizer, and it is found on the white "mountains" that emerge from the Pacific. Mountain sacrifice scenes link blood to mountain runoff, as the objective of making such sacrifices was likely to induce or perpetuate the flow of water, and the stream of blood links the mountain to the basin. The polysemous elements of this metaphorical domain were, to a degree, interchangeable in imagery and ritual, and served as potent examples of what Tilley (1999) terms "solid" or "material metaphors," which differ from linguistic metaphors in that they have material substance and can be manipulated in social and ritual contexts and in turn, convey deeper meanings to and shape those contexts through their inalienable qualities and the meanings ascribed to them.

---

[21] Malting, the conversion of starches into sugars by germinating maize kernels, is a method of preparing maize for fermentation that does not involve saliva. Moore (1989: 686) reports the presence of germinated maize in association with *chicha*-making implements at the Late Intermediate period North Coast site of Manchan.

Furthermore, material metaphors tend to accumulate or condense meanings more readily than linguistic metaphors (Tilley 1999: 263).

If the Moche shared the common view in the Andes of the cosmos as a series of nested forms with the human body as its basis, human fertility can be viewed as a microcosm of larger-scale phenomena such as agricultural and environmental cycles. In this view, the organizing principles of a right and left side or an upper and lower portion are opposed, but mediated to make a complementary whole. Fluid is the medium that integrates and animates solid forms and oppositional entities. Water circulates between the mountains and the coastal huaca centers and integrates the landscape, just as circulating fluids integrate the organs of the body. The movement of fluid between the mountains and the coast and among and between bodies is the essence of the Andean hydraulic cycle. Through the movement of fluid from the mountains to the coast, fields are fertilized. During sexual intercourse, fluids circulate and intermingle, fertilizing the womb. Offerings of blood or *chicha* give potency to actions and events. This series of relationships is manifest in the Larco Jar, which illustrates a cosmological charter for the integration of the mountains and the coast through the copulation of a mountain deity and a coastal woman or deity, and the integration of male and female through sexual reproduction. For the Inca, the act of offering a cup of *chicha* to someone else and drinking the other "served to integrate separate bodies through a sharing of fluids" (Classen 1993: 59). It is possible that *chicha* may have integrated Moche social and physical bodies as well. The similarity in form shared between the Larco Jar and the vessel(s) in which the liquid is prepared and poured on its scene suggests that it was used as a *chicha* vessel. The Larco Jar itself may have served the function of integrating members of society through drink, or perhaps mediating between the living and the deceased as a funerary offering.

Analysis of the imagery on the Larco Jar suggests that it relates a mythological narrative involving Wrinkle Face, a mountain deity, and his sexual encounter with a woman on the coast. The narrative was enriched and made tangible through visual metaphors that conflate mountain run-off, *chicha*, guano, and semen, and ties the Andean hydraulic system, involving the cycling of water to the coast from the mountains, to human sexuality. Mountains were associated with masculinity, and the river valleys that are fertilized by water from the mountains to yield crops, are feminine. In this way, the human act of procreation is a microcosmic event that is echoed in broader cosmological phenomena that are necessary for survival on the arid coast.

The apparent role of huaca centers was to ensure the flow of water to the coast through ceremony and mediation with distant mountains. While Huacas de Moche was the backdrop for such ceremonies, the workshop at the huaca center produced permanent works which made visible the *modus operandi* behind natural forces that impact the lives of followers of Moche religion, thus perpetuating and disseminating myths involving the relationship of the coast and the mountains. Artists producing tangible, enduring objects at Huacas de Moche supported and solidified the function of the huaca center through the use of a symbolic visual system that could be understood by adherents of Moche religion.

Chapter 5:
Ancestry and Agricultural Fertility

Benson (1997a: 45, 2012: 69) suggests that scenes which depict Wrinkle Face copulating with a woman represent the origin of the Moche people. Comparison of the Larco Jar's narrative scene with other Moche examples lends support to her hypothesis, and indicates that Moche artists symbolically linked Wrinkle Face to broader Andean notions of ancestry, mortality, and agricultural fertility. Not only does the Larco Jar reflect a deliberate effort to integrate the Moche religious system into a preexisting Andean worldview, but it also did so in visual language that was new and, in essence, balanced novelty and innovation with tradition and familiarity. The political motivation behind promoting Wrinkle Face as a paramount ancestor may have been to unite otherwise disparate kin groups under an inclusive religion with Huacas de Moche as its focal point.

On the Larco Jar and other similar examples, it is not clear whether the structure in which Wrinkle Face copulates is open on the sides or if it is enclosed, providing the viewer with an X-ray perspective (figure 4.1). The stirrup-spout vessel near the heads of Wrinkle Face and his consort may be hung on the wall behind them, may be placed on the floor next to them through "stacking" as a means of representing depth of field, or may float above them as an ideographic symbol, adding emphasis, clarification, or additional information to the scene. The point at which the anterior post of the structure would meet the foundation cannot be seen.

Perhaps owing to Western conventions of the portrayal of spatial depth in two dimensions, previous studies have overlooked the fact that Wrinkle Face is an integral part of the structure, and the post is not behind him, but rather emerges from his lower back. As discussed in Chapter 2, Moche artists occasionally employed depth of field in vase painting by stacking objects vertically, as exemplified in the hills in figure 2.1. However, the overlapping of images to show spatial depth does not appear to have been a widely used method in the Moche visual system. In two similar examples that were not likely produced by the same artist that made the Larco Jar, the post is clearly part of Wrinkle Face's headdress (figures 4.2 & 4.3). On the Larco Jar and other similar examples in which the post is not integrated into Wrinkle Face's

headdress, it is therefore likely that the base of the wooden post is "watered" by the liquid poured by the bird. Furthermore, the placement of the post near the genitals of the copulating pair suggests that it may grow from the fertilizing act of intercourse.

The house scene is strikingly similar to imagery on two unprovenienced Phase IV vessels (figures 4.4 & 4.5), in which Wrinkle Face copulates with a woman beneath a tree (Hocquenghem and Golte 1987: 278), and they may represent a similar mythical tale, an alternate portrayal of the same episode, or more likely a temporal or regional variant of the same myth. In both examples, a tree, rather than a house post, appears to sprout from Wrinkle Face's lower back as he copulates (Bergh 1993: 84; Golte 2009: 64). A gold and silver nose ornament from Tomb 9 of Sipán (figure 4.6; Alva 2001: 238) appears to confirm that the tree grows from Wrinkle Face, and suggests that similar beliefs may have been held in the northern Moche region. On the nose ornament, trees emerge from the backs of the two prone figures, roots are visible beneath their waists, and fruits or leaves, attached with rings, hang freely from the branches. The figures' grimacing mouths and feline headdresses warrant their identification as Wrinkle Face. The placement of the trees in relation to the prone figures parallels that of the tree that appears to sprout from Wrinkle Face's back in copulation scenes and the house post in the Larco Jar and other similar examples.

In a fine-line example of the copulation scene in which a tree sprouts from Wrinkle Face's back (figure 4.5), he is accompanied by cast of zoomorphic characters similar to those shown on the Larco Jar. Iguana and an anthropomorphic mammal (probably a fox, based on similarity to other Moche depictions) sit cross-legged with hands clasped next to the copulating pair. Two fragmentary anthropomorphic birds are situated above Iguana and the mammal. A dog stands beneath the serpent belt of Wrinkle Face, and the deity grasps a fruit with his outstretched hand as he couples with a woman. A plant grows next to the head of the woman, and a *florero* (flaring bowl), a stirrup-spout vessel, and three *espingo* seeds are placed immediately above the plant. It is noteworthy that the vessels appear next to the heads of the copulating pair, similar to the placement of

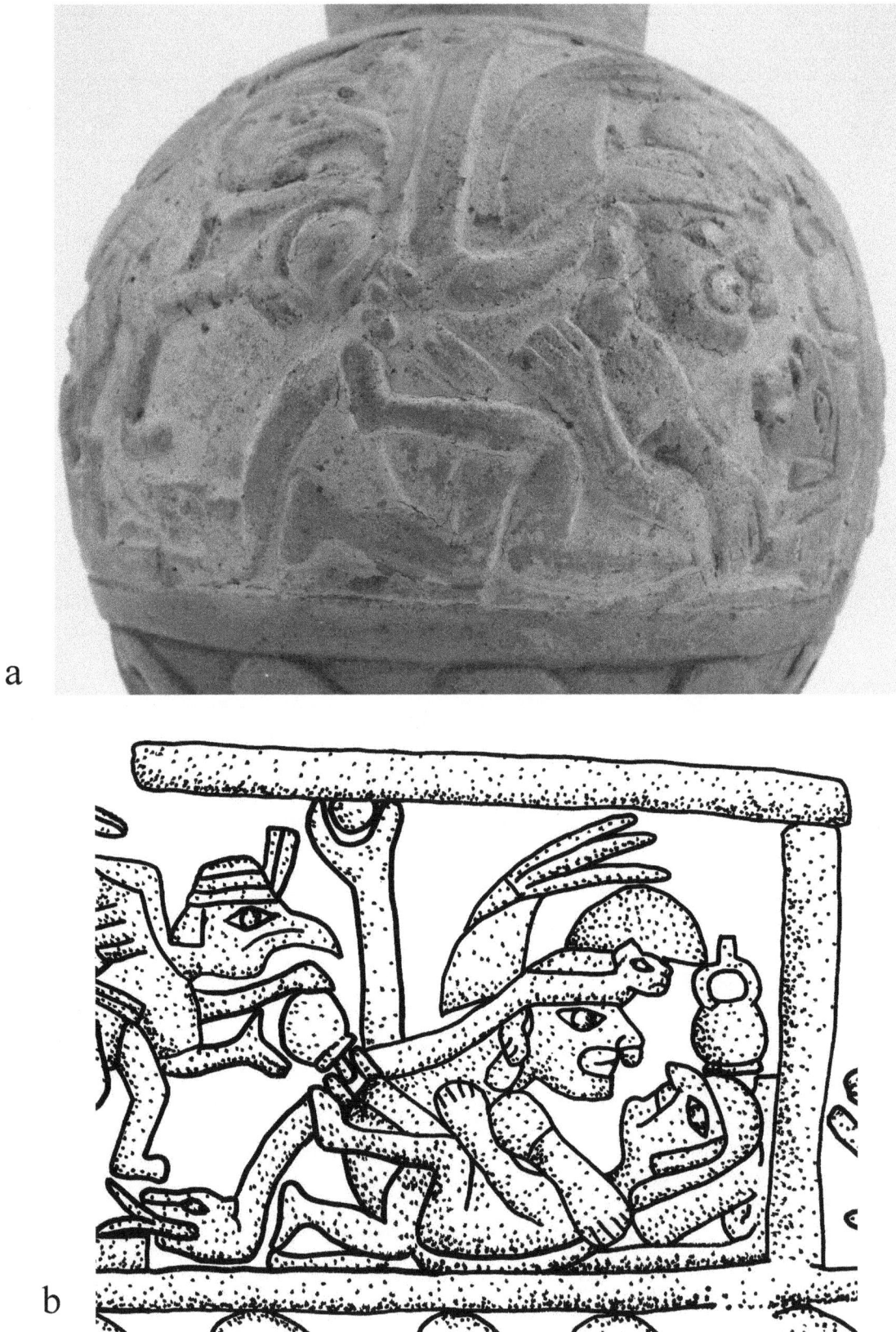

Figure 5.1. Depictions of Wrinkle Face with a house post emerging from his back: a) Jar with low-relief copulation scene (detail). Museo Larco, Lima. ML004365; b) Rollout drawing of jar found in Huaca de la Luna Plaza 1 (detail). After drawing by Jorge Sachún.

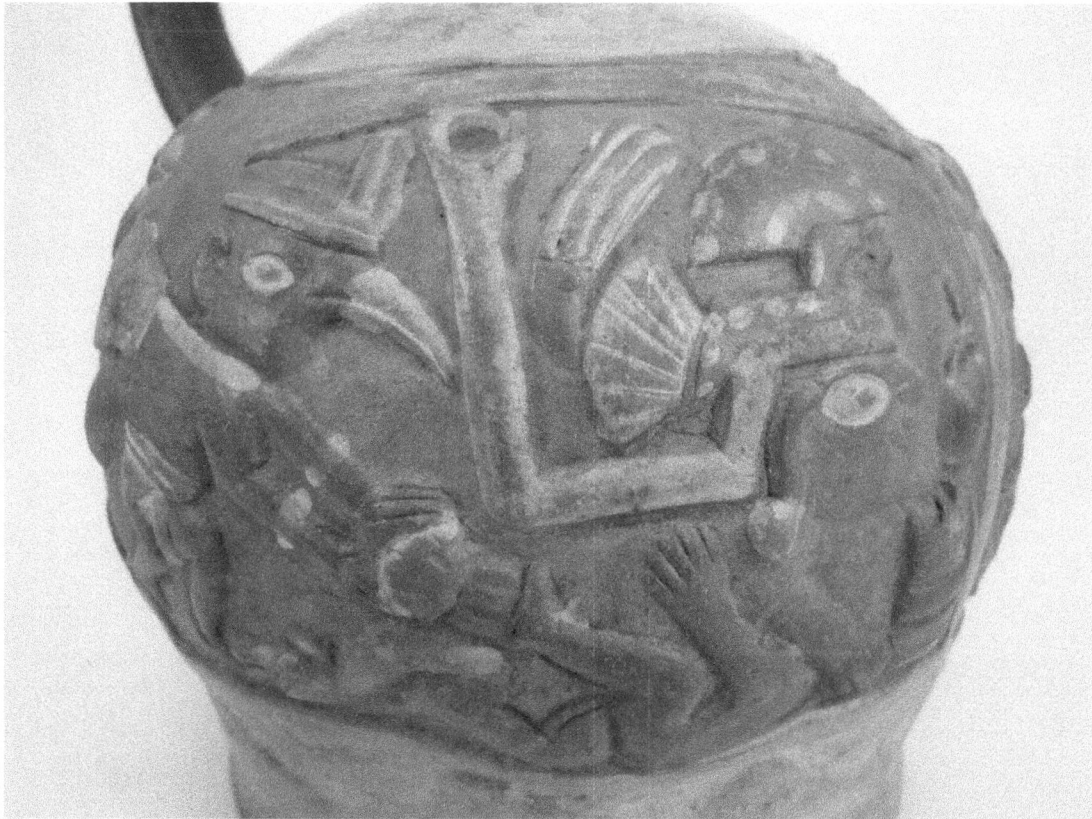

Figure 5.2. Spout-and-handle vessel with low-relief copulation scene (detail).
Museo Larco, Lima. ML004358.

Figure 5.3. Rollout drawing of low-relief copulation scene (detail).
British Museum, London. After Donnan 1976: fig. 1.

a

b

c

Figure 5.4: a) Low-relief spout-and-handle vessel portraying copulation scene and tree. Museo Larco, Lima. ML004359; b) Tree and Wrinkle Face copulating with woman (detail); c) Rollout drawing of low relief scene. After drawing by Percy Fiestas.

Figure 5.5: a) Stirrup-spout fine-line vessel with copulation scene and tree. After Donnan and McClelland 1999: fig. 4.96; b) Rollout drawing of fine-line copulation scene on stirrup-spout vessel. After drawing by Donna McClelland.

Figure 5.6. Tree figures from gold and silver nose ornament from Tomb 9 of Sipán. Museo Tumbas Reales de Sipán, Lambayeque, Peru. After Alva 2001: fig. 23.

the stirrup-spout bottle placed near the couple's heads on the Larco Jar. In this instance, there is no wall upon which the vessels could be hung, suggesting that they could be ideographs. It is equally likely that the vessels were intended to be read as sitting on the ground near the heads of the couple, but the artist chose this method of representation in order to convey the most information to the viewer. Monkeys wearing bags gather comma-shaped fruit (referred to as *ulluchu*) that grow from the tree.[22] Behind the copulating pair and the sprouting tree, four humans with bags are surrounded by *ulluchu* fruits, and two of them kneel next to a mound-shaped object filled with small semicircular forms that they probe with thin sticks. This may be an oven in which they are roasting seeds or fruit, and the scene may parallel the liquid preparation undertaken by birds in the scenes in which Wrinkle Face copulates within the structure.

The *ulluchu* appears frequently in the art of Phases III, IV, and V (McClelland 2008: 43), yet its significance is poorly understood, and the identity of the plant has proven difficult to ascertain.[23]

---

[22] On the nose ornament from Sipán (figure 4.6), the comma-shaped fruit hang with their bulbous ends up, unlike other depictions of *ulluchu*. The tree may represent a different species, however the artist may have inverted the fruit in order to better accommodate the metal rings from which they hang.

---

[23] Larco (1939: 98) dubbed the plant "ulluchu" and claimed to have identified the fruit as an edible species found in the sierras. Larco's identification was never verified (see McClelland 1977). The *ulluchu*'s association with scenes of sacrifice has been explained through identification as *Carica candicans*, a wild papaya that contains the enzyme papain that was hypothetically used during the bleeding of captives to prevent blood from coagulating during the Sacrifice Ceremony (Hultin *et al.* 1987). Bussmann and Sharon (2009: 3) argue against identification of the *ulluchu* as *Carica candicans*, and they do not believe that the wild papaya was collected for use as an anticoagulant because domesticated papaya was common among the Moche and would have been easier to harvest for the same purpose. Alva (2001: 244, footnote 3) believes that the *ulluchu* was not a papaya, but rather belongs to the family Meliaceae, as do Bussmann and Sharon (2009: 5) who attribute it to the genus *Guarea*, from the family Meliaceae, based on its appearance and possible attributes. When inhaled, *Guarea* seeds may cause hallucinations and can cause heightened blood pressure, increased heartbeat, and widened blood vessels, which could both cause erections and aid in blood extraction (Bussmann and Sharon 2009: 6). According to McClelland (2008: 62), *ulluchu* is probably too small to be Meliaceae. Depictions in art suggest that the *ulluchu* fruit is 4 to 6 inches long, although scale is not used consistently in Moche representations (McClelland 1977: 439). Actual *ulluchu* specimens have been found in excavations, and they are much smaller than they appear in Moche representations, roughly 1 inch or so. A banner found in Tomb 3 of Sipán contained actual *ulluchu* fruit encased between metal forms and a textile backing (Alva 2001: 227, 231), but they could not be recovered, nor could samples from a cache at Sipán (McClelland 2008: 59). *Ulluchus* have also been found scattered near the right side of a buried giant male at Dos Cabezas

Diagnostic features of the *ulluchu* are the comma-shaped body which is usually striated, and a round calyx (McClelland 2008: 43). In Moche representations, monkeys are generally associated with *ulluchus* (McClelland 1977: 449, 2008: 63), and *ulluchu* is the only fruit that is shown being collected in Moche art. The *ulluchu* does not appear to denote a specific location or environment (McClelland 1977: 441). Most *ulluchus* are portrayed with deities (see for example figure 1.7; McClelland 1977: 443), although it does not appear to be exclusively associated with any particular deity; if one supernatural being in a scene has an *ulluchu*, then others usually do as well (McClelland 1977: 449). Authors have suggested that the fruit was used in sacrificial ceremonies (e.g. Hultin, *et al.* 1987), but Quilter argues that *ulluchu* may rather "indicate a sacred state rather than being specifically tied to sacrifice" (Quilter 1990: 57). Bussmann and Sharon (2009: 4-5) suggest that *ulluchu* use may have caused sexual arousal, due to its presence in sex scenes and association with ithyphallic captives on the frieze at Huaca Cao Viejo. Such a reading would not be inconsistent with Wrinkle Face copulation scenes, although given the variety of contexts in which the fruit appears, it probably carried additional meanings and/or functions.

Aside from its association with deities, the *ulluchu* may carry masculine or phallic connotations. In Moche art, the shape of the *ulluchu* is reminiscent of a penis and scrotum. *Ulluchus* are also occasionally placed between the legs of Moche warriors in fine-line depictions. In figure 4.7, an *ulluchu* beneath a victorious warrior is juxtaposed with the exposed member that hangs between the legs of his stripped and bound captive. On the low-relief copulation scene which portrays a tree sprouting from Wrinkle Face's back, curved *ulluchus* grow from one half of the tree and round, and cleft *espingos* from the other (figure 4.4b; McClelland 2008: 58). In this instance, the tree, which sprouts from the union of the couple and produces two types of fruit, may mediate or unify the masculine/feminine pairing. *Espingos,* which resemble coffee beans in Moche art, are identifiable as cotyledons from the genus *Nectandra* (Towle 1961: 40), which may have been used as a psychotropic and mixed with *chicha* (Wassén 1976). In the fine-line example in figure 4.5, Wrinkle Face "points" an *ulluchu* at three *espingos*

(Donnan 2007: 119; McClelland 2008: 61). According to Quilter (pers. comm. 2012), *ulluchu* fruit are from mangrove swamps of coastal Ecuador, but this requires further investigation.

as he copulates, lending further phallic connotation to the *ulluchu*, and suggesting that the *espingo* may symbolically represent a vulva, which it resembles in form as depicted in Moche art.

Figure 5.7. Fine-line depiction of warrior and captive (detail). After drawing by Donna McClelland.

Beyond their similar placement at the lower back of Wrinkle Face on the Larco Jar, the fine-line vessel, and the Sipán nose ornament, the house post and tree may be symbolically related in Moche thought. As previously noted, on the Larco Jar, the anthropomorphic bird with the fisher headdress pours a concoction onto the copulating pair that can metaphorically be considered mountain run-off water, semen, *chicha*, and guano through their metaphorical relationship as white, fertilizing fluids. *Chicha* is a product of a successful harvest, and is commonly consumed during harvest celebrations in the Andes. For the Inca, the relationship of *chicha* to agricultural fertility is made apparent in a ceramic object known as a *paccha*, which combines a foot plow, an ear of maize, and an *urpu*, the imperial Inca vessel used for storing and serving *chicha*. The *paccha*, which was likely used for pouring *chicha* offerings in fields, presents all of the pivotal phases of agriculture simultaneously, as the digging stick refers to planting, the maize ear to cultivation, and the *urpu* to harvest and transformation into *chicha* (Stone-Miller 2002: 254-257).

Growing crops and raising house posts could be considered analogous practices. *Chicha* is also commonly poured ceremonially on and around house posts during house-building in the Andes (e.g. Arnold 1991), and the pouring of *chicha* by the bird on the Larco Jar may be viewed as a foundational libation. Guano was probably used as a crop fertilizer by the Moche (Benson 1972: 78, 1995: 250; Larco Hoyle 1946: 163), as suggested by the interest they took in guano islands. The pre-Hispanic Inca were known to have visited guano islands, and coastal peoples under Inca rule made use of guano as crop fertilizer. According to the chronicler Cieza de León:

> Out of the sea, in the neighborhood of these valleys, rise some islands much frequented by seals. The natives go to them in *balsas*, and bring a great quantity of the dung of birds from the rocks, to apply to their crops of maize, and they find it so efficacious that the land, which formerly was sterile, becomes very rich and fruitful. If they cease to use this manure, they reap little maize. Indeed the people could not be supported if the birds, lodging on the rocks round these islands, did not leave that which is afterwards collected, and considered so valuable as to become an article of trade between the natives (1964: 265-266).

The value of guano as a fertilizer may have led Moche elites to attempt to control or regulate its distribution and incorporate guano-related symbolism into Moche ideology. Around the time of the Spanish Conquest, guano was considered such an important commodity that Inca rulers sought to control its distribution and protect the islands. Garcilaso de la Vega adds:

> On the sea coast from below Arequipa to Tarapaca, a distance of more than two hundred leagues, they use no other manure than the droppings of sea birds, of which there are large and small along all the coast, and they fly in such enormous flocks that it would be incredible to any one who had not seen them. They breed on certain desert islands on the coast, and the quantity of manure they make is also incredible. From a distance these heaps of manure look like the peaks of snowy mountains. In the time of the Kings Yncas [*sic*] such care was taken to preserve these birds that it was unlawful for any one to land on the islands during the breeding season on pain of death; that the birds might not be

disturbed or driven from their nests (1960: 11).

Given that the Moche revered guano islands and the likelihood that the Moche also used guano as fertilizer for crops, the concoction prepared and poured by the guano birds on the Larco Jar can be viewed as a fertilizer for the wooden house post that grows from Wrinkle Face as he copulates.

It is probable that part of the significance of guano islands is in their similarity to mountains, and they may have played a crucial role in the hydraulic cycle. Covered in white guano, the islands superficially resemble miniature versions of the peaks of the snowy Cordillera Blanca, the ultimate source of irrigation water on the Andean coast. Dean (2006a: 112-113) observes that for the Inca, "echo stones," such as the well-known Funerary Rock at Machu Picchu, served as metonymous surrogates for distant mountains. In other words, giving offerings to an echo stone was a substitute for taking offerings to distant *apus*, of which they were considered a smaller part. In a similar vein to Tilley's (1999) material metaphors, Dean describes material metonymy as "a relationship of parts, in which one thing that is perceived to be a part of the second thing, substitutes for it" (2006a: 106). Evidence of material metonymy in regard to Moche beliefs concerning mountains is found at Huacas de Moche. Plaza 3A of Huaca de la Luna, located at the foot of Cerro Blanco, yielded the remains of more than seventy sacrificed individuals (Bourget 1997, 1998, 2001). The dominant feature of Plaza 3A is the large stone that is enshrined within it and may have been a "reduced image" of Cerro Blanco and an object of veneration to which the sacrifices were offered (Bourget 1997; Uceda 2000: 93).

The wooden house post and the tree that grow from Wrinkle Face's back in depictions are analogous because they share material substance, despite different surface appearances. Wood was undoubtedly a scarce and precious material for the Moche, as suggested by the relative lack of wooden objects known from excavations at Moche sites versus the relatively high number of Moche wooden sculptures left as offerings on guano islands. While acknowledging that house posts and trees are similar in that they are both made of wood may be a simplistic observation, the relationship between materiality and surface appearance is often a complex matter in the Andes. Dean (2006a: 105) notes that, for the Inca, the substance of an object was of greater importance than its outer appearance. For example, stone was a highly significant material

Figure 5.8. Rollout drawing of low-relief scene with Botanical Frog on spout-and-handle bottle. After drawing by Donna McClelland.

and it is not clear that they valued worked stone over unworked rock (Dean 2006a, 2006b: 29). In corporeal terms, royal fingernails and hair were treated with great care and were viewed as material metonyms for the ruler (see Betanzos 1996: 205; Dean 2006a: 109; Salomon 1995: 332), suggesting that human sheddings retained the body's essence, even after separation from the body (Lau 2008: 1033). *Qeros*, wooden ceremonial drinking cups that were exchanged in feasts and ceremonies, were made in pairs from the same block of wood (Cummins 2004: 7), which suggests that they retained a mutual essence of the parent tree after being carved. Two drinkers sharing a toast with a pair of *qeros* were bonded through a common essence by imbibing *chicha*, but likely also through the use of paired vessels that shared the essence of the tree from which they were hewn. Similarly, a house post carved from a tree may have retained its arboreal essence in Moche thought, despite the change in context and appearance, as suggested by the compositional and contextual similarities between the house post and tree that grow from Wrinkle Face's back in copulation scenes.

For the Moche, evidence suggests that the inner material essence of an object was at least as important as surface appearance. A frieze at Huaca Cao Viejo, a site that shares strong affinities with Huacas de Moche and may have been in its sphere of influence, depicts a row of frontally rendered male figures that link hands and wear tunics, ear spools, and headdresses. The feet of one of the figures has chipped away, revealing human and llama bones placed into the wall beneath the painted and stuccoed surface (Verano and Anderson 1996, cited in Gálvez Mora and Briceño Rosario 2001: 152). The bones would not have been visible to viewers, yet their placement beneath the surface likely imbued the frieze with potency or essence. Moche metallurgists also developed highly specialized gilding and silvering techniques that allude to the importance of the unseen internal substance of objects. While they could have simply gilded or silvered the surface of a more common or less valuable material, Moche metallurgists opted to use the labor-intensive process of depletion gilding (or depletion silvering), which involves the production of an object in gold- or silver-copper alloy, which is then repeatedly bathed in acids to remove the copper from the outer surface, thus enriching the surface and giving the object the appearance of pure gold or silver (Lechtman 1979: 29, 1996: 39-41; Pasztory 1997: 63-64). The use of depletion gilding and silvering suggests that the internal essences of gold or silver were significant. Lechtman notes:

> The basis of Andean enrichment systems is the incorporation of the essential ingredient into the very body of the object. The essence of the object, that which appears superficially to be true of it, must also be inside of it. The object is not that object unless it contains within it the essential quality, even if the essence is only minimally present. For, without the incorporation of the essence, its visual manifestation is impossible. (1979: 32)

Like Moche enriched gold and silver objects, it is probable that the essence of wood was highly valued, whether the surface form was that of a tree, sculpture, or house post.

An additional scene, known from four Moche Phase IV spout-and-handle vessels, shows an episode related to Wrinkle Face's copulation scenes (figure 4.8), and thematically concerns harvest (Carrión Cachot 1959: 129-131) and agricultural bounty (McClelland 2011: 40), featuring maize and beans. Like the Larco Jar, Wrinkle Face, Iguana, anthropomorphic birds, and the dog are present. In the lower register, a row of monkeys, followed by a

Figure 5.9. Representations of the Botanical Frog: a) Botanical Frog from low-relief spout-and-handle bottle (detail). After drawing by Donna McClelland; b) Anthropomorphized Botanical Frog from fineline vessel. After drawing by Donna McClelland; c) Stirrup-spout vessel formed as Botanical Frog. Museo Larco, Lima; d) Fine-line scene on Munich Vessel (detail). After Quilter 1997: fig. 2.

zoomorphic animal with a looped object that is probably a whip, carry net bags. The bags are likely full of *ulluchus* collected from the tree that grew from Wrinkle Face's back as he copulated with his female consort, suggesting that the harvest scene follows the copulation scene as part of a larger mythical narrative involving Wrinkle Face, Iguana, the anthropomorphic birds, and the monkeys. Furthermore, the bags, slung over the monkeys' shoulders, are roughly shaped like *ulluchus*, recalling the form of the fruit, and the anthropomorphic bird at the front of the row likely also holds an *ulluchu*. Two anthropomorphic birds and the dog stand next to a U-shaped bicephalic serpent that encloses ears of maize and a figure identifiable as Wrinkle Face, based on his serpent belt and association with the other characters. In the same register as the U-shaped bicephalic serpent, Wrinkle Face is portrayed again and points to a square arrangement of maize while holding an *ulluchu* aloft, and Iguana stands behind him next to an assortment of beans while holding a spout-and-handle vessel in one hand and his exposed member in the other.[24] The appearance of Wrinkle Face twice suggests that the scene represents a sequential narrative.

A chimerical beast with plants sprouting from its body that is not known to appear with Wrinkle Face and Iguana in other contexts is rendered prominently in the Harvest Scene (figures 4.8 & 4.9a). McClelland (2011) has dubbed this creature (also referred to as the Jaguar-Toad) the "Botanical Frog," and notes that it is typically represented as a frog with a feline snout and ears, striped front legs, clawed feet, and manioc on its back, and may also have manioc stalks as horns or on its spine, tubers in the corner of its mouth, and beans on its body (McClelland 2011: 30-31).[25] The appearance of the Botanical Frog, covered with edible plants, is consistent with interpretation of the scene as related to harvest and agricultural bounty, as it appears to be a physical embodiment of root crops.

The Botanical Frog only appears in certain contexts. In a unique Phase IV fine-line example, the Botanical Frog is painted as an anthropomorphized warrior in a procession of other animal warriors that carry a figure referred to as the Rayed God (or Warrior Priest) in a litter (figure 4.9b; Donnan 1996: fig. 4.107; McClelland 2011: 36-37). The Rayed God is the recipient of sacrificial blood in the Presentation Theme, but the scene with the anthropomorphic Botanical Frog is a likely precursor to or a fragment of the Revolt of the Objects. The Revolt of the Objects is represented by a series of scenes in which zoomorphic warriors and humans battle against animated weaponry and other accouterments of warfare, and the Rayed God is a central protagonist.[26] The sequence was also writ large in a now-destroyed mural at Huaca de la Luna (Quilter 1990: 44).

In addition to the fine-line scene and the Harvest Scene examples, McClelland (2011: 30) notes that the Botanical Frog is the subject of twenty-four sculptural Moche vessels. Of the sculptural examples of the Botanical Frog, most represent the solitary beast in a crouched position (figure 4.9c), although in some instances it copulates with a jaguar, which may relate to Wrinkle Face, given his jaguar-like traits such as his feline headdress and fangs.[27] When the Botanical Frog copulates with a feline, it does so in a face-to-face non-naturalistic manner that otherwise only appears in Moche depictions of human intercourse (McClelland 2011: 33).

The Botanical Frog may be associated with Wrinkle Face in one other instance. A small Botanical Frog, identifiable by the manioc tubers that hang from its back, faces a figure beneath a tree in an example of the Revolt of the Objects on the well-known Munich Vessel (figure 4.10; McClelland 2011: 41). The anthropomorphic figure wears a stepped tunic

---

[24] As in the example illustrated in figure 4.7, the *ulluchu* is juxtaposed with the male sex organ in the Harvest Scene, as they are both held in the right hands of Wrinkle Face and Iguana, respectively. Also of note, the spout-and-handle vessel held in Iguana's left hand occurs in a scene that strongly relates to the harvest of agricultural produce. This suggests that the contents of the vessel are in fact *chicha*, which is a product of harvest and is widely consumed in modern harvest celebrations in rural communities in the Andes. One might consider the possibility that Iguana is drunk in this scene.

[25] McClelland (2011) has written extensively on the Botanical Frog and has identified it as *Leptodactylus pentadactylus*, a frog native to the eastern Andean forest, but not to the Moche region. She notes that like the manioc tubers that hang from the Botanical Frog's back, *L. pentadactylus* is poisonous and, furthermore, manioc tubers can be stored underground for years, which may relate to the frog's ability to burrow for long periods of time during dry seasons. Feline-like characteristics of *L. pentadactylus* include similar markings, claw-like digits, and a cat-like scream.

[26] Quilter (1990) interprets the Revolt of the Objects as a mythical narrative, perhaps a variant of one recorded in the Colonial-period Huarochirí Manuscript in which traditional roles of people and objects were reversed with violent consequences at the end of a previous age before the current order was established. Similar stories are common in Native American myth systems.

[27] In other instances, a jaguar copulates with a relatively naturalistic toad. Larco Hoyle (1965: 105) views toad/jaguar copulation as a union of water (represented by the toad) and earth (represented by the jaguar), and the Botanical Frog (laden with agricultural produce) as the product of this union.

Figure 5.10. Botanical Frog and tree figure from Munich Vessel (detail).
After Quilter 1997: fig. 2.

and may indeed be Wrinkle Face. It is unclear whether the figure is seated under the tree, or if the roots of the tree are emanating from him (Quilter 1990: 53), but the placement of the roots and trunk of the fruit-laden tree near the figure's lower back and genitals is reminiscent of the tree that sprouts from Wrinkle Face in copulation scenes (figures 4.4 & 4.5) and the gold and silver nose ornament from Sipán (figure 4.6). Furthermore, the tree represented on the Munich Vessel may be an *ulluchu* (Quilter 1997: 27). Although the fruit are slightly different in shape, likely owing to the minute scale of the painting on the Munich Vessel, the pinnate leaves of the tree are similar to those on the tree that sprouts from Wrinkle Face's back, illustrated in figure 4.5b. If my identification of the figure as Wrinkle Face is correct, his copulation scenes and the Harvest Scene may be anchored to the Revolt of the Objects as part of a yet larger mythical narrative.[28]

The seated figure on the Munich Vessel that I suspect is Wrinkle Face may represent a Moche rendition of a tree-person, or *mallki* (Hocquenghem 1989: 171).[29] Although little is known about the *ulluchu*, it is significant that it is a fruit-bearing tree that grows from Wrinkle Face's back. "Mallki," in

Quechua, can be defined as "young plant," "fruit tree," "cultivated tree," or "the body of an ancestor" (Classen 1993: 24; Isbell 1978: 147; Sherbondy 1986). With roots in the earth and branches bearing fruit akin to offspring, ancestors are often conceived of as trees or likened to them through metaphor in the Andes (Classen 1993: 24; DeLeonardis and Lau 2004: 80; Lau 2008: 1033). Trees link ancestors and the living because their roots grow into the ground, the domain of the deceased, and they grow through the world of the living. Similarly, in Inca thought, ancestors emerged to the surfaces of the lands they inhabited through tree roots, caves, and springs (Hastorf and Johannessen 1991: 153). In the Colonial-period Huarochirí Manuscript, ancestors emerged from a quinoa plant, and other people came from the fruit of a tree (Huarochirí Manuscript 1991: 117; 119). *Buddleia* (the butterfly bush) was symbolically valued by the Inca and may have been associated with the ancestral line (Hastorf and Johannessen 1991: 150-151). The *huarango* (a tree from the genus *Prosopis* that bears edible fruit, also called *algarrobo* on the North Coast) may have been associated with lineage groups and *mallkis* on the pre-Hispanic South Coast (Beresford-Jones 2011: 118; Silverman 1993: 193). The wide distribution of such beliefs across the Andes suggests the likelihood that the Moche may have held similar conceptions of ancestry and lineage in relation to fruit-bearing trees.

Metaphors for ancestors involving vegetative fertility are pervasive in Colonial and contemporary

---

[28] Quilter (1990; 1997) links the Revolt of the Objects to other scenes such as the Boat Theme and Presentation Theme and views them as fragments of a single narrative.

[29] For additional possible Moche examples of tree-people, see Benson (2012: 35).

mortuary practices and beliefs (Salomon 1995: 340-341), and ancestors are widely associated with seeds and cultigens in the Andes. Contemporary and ethnohistoric accounts link the transformation of the body that occurs through aging and death to agricultural and hydraulic metaphors. Death is a transformative process, and can be viewed as a separation of wet and dry, and a "drying up" of the body (Classen 1993: 15). Human beings begin life wet and soft, and over a lifetime dry out and harden until they become a seed- or tree-like *mallki* (Salomon 1991: 16, 1995: 328). In essence, the practice of placing mummy bundles in the ground is akin to planting seeds (DeLeonardis and Lau 2004: 102-103; Frame 1995: 14, 2001: 71; Lau 2008: 1033). The relationship between mortuary bundles and seeds can be traced back to an Early Horizon Paracas Necropolis bundle which contained a large bag of beans, rather than a corpse, and may relate to the regenerative and reproductive abilities of ancestors when buried (DeLeonardis and Lau 2004: 103; Frame 2001: 71-72). Paracas Necropolis embroidered textiles, found as wrappings on mortuary bundles, are also frequently decorated with figures that may be ancestors who sprout plants and seeds, including beans, tubers, maize, and other cultigens (Frame 2001: 69-72).

Figure 5.11. Jar representing maize and head of deity. Museo de Arqueología, Antropología e Historia de la Universidad Nacional de Trujillo, Trujillo, Peru.

In several other instances, Wrinkle Face transforms into a plant, or displays botanical characteristics that may further relate to his identity as a *mallki*. In some sculptural vessels, the face of a fanged deity that could be Wrinkle Face is sometimes represented among ears of maize, some molded from actual cobs (figure 4.11; see Eubanks 1999: 33-73). Significantly, Wrinkle Face is also linked to maize in the Harvest Scene. As an important staple crop, maize, like fruit trees, may have been associated with *mallkis*. Some vessels represent Wrinkle Face with his body replaced by manioc tubers (see Quilter 2010: 98-99), and manioc stalks occasionally sprout from his head (figure 4.12a). His transfiguration as a manioc may portray him as a *mallki*, and suggests an episode that may be related to the Harvest Scene and the Botanical Frog. Manioc is an important tropical root crop at lower elevations, and interestingly, Sillar (1996: 269) argues that freeze-drying potatoes in the highlands is akin to the act of mummification. Similarly, Lau (2008: 1035) relates Late Horizon funerary structures called *chullpas* to storehouses known as *collcas* because *chullpas* stored dried, desiccated ancestors, and *collcas* analogously stored freeze-dried potatoes. Salomon (1995: 321) notes that smaller chambers that held mummified remains were also called *collcas*.

It is noteworthy that in the example illustrated in figure 4.12a, in which Wrinkle Face's body is replaced by manioc tubers, he makes half-fist gestures with his hands, a gesture related to male sexual fertility and mountains. Another unique vessel is modeled as a supine, fanged deity who may be Wrinkle Face (figure 4.13). His body resembles a tuber, and the vessel has a large phallic spout which may have been used to receive libations if the vessels was buried in a floor with the spout exposed (Quilter 2010: 124). Quilter notes that it may have been placed similarly to a vessel shaped like the head of an owl that was found above the tomb of the Señora de Cao at Huaca Cao Viejo, and was presumably for receiving liquid offerings (see Mujica Barreda, *et al.* 2007: 210-211). Moche burial practices differ from those of many other Andean cultures in that Moche corpses were typically placed in tombs supine, rather than flexed or seated, and the ancestral body may have been likened to a manioc tuber or other root crop, as suggested by the tuber-shaped vessel with a phallic spout. Vessels in which Wrinkle Face's body is replaced by a tuber suggest conceptual similarity to the potato- or beanlike ancestors of other cultures in the Andes.

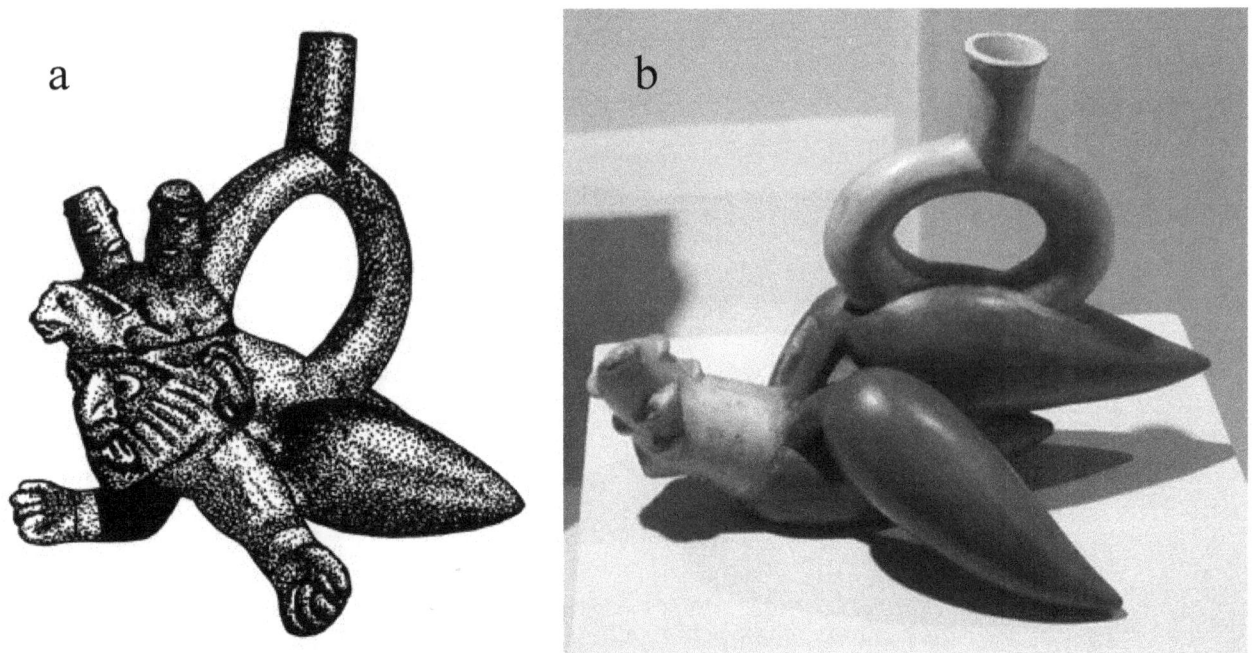

Figure 5.12. Vessels in the form of manioc plants: a) Stirrup-spout vessel in the form of Wrinkle Face and manioc. After Donnan 1976: fig. 100; b) Vessel in the form of a manioc plant. Museo Nacional de Arqueología Antropología e Historia del Perú, Lima.

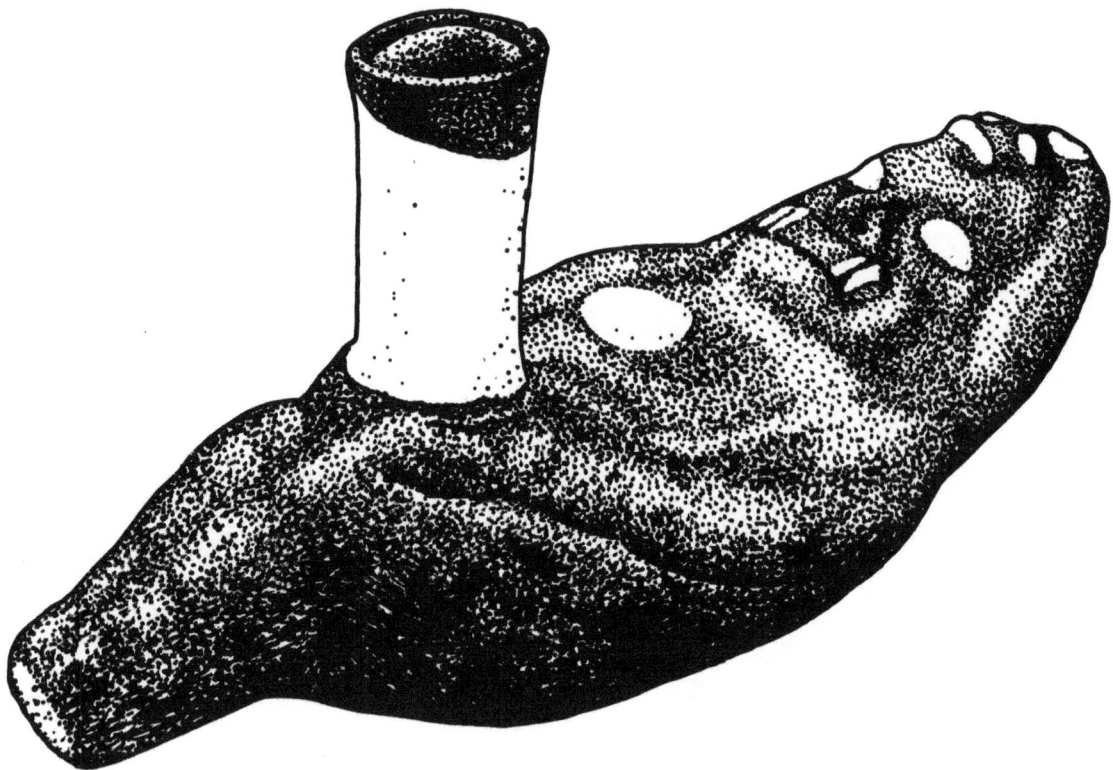

Figure 5.13. Vessel in the form of a recumbent male. After Quilter 2010: Plate 17.

The conceptualization of ancestors as fruit-bearing trees, seeds, beans, and tubers in the Andes denotes the direct and ongoing role they play in providing and ensuring agricultural fertility. The establishment of irrigation systems, fields, and villages, and the introduction of certain crops are often attributed to important ancestors (DeLeonardis and Lau 2004: 79; Lau 2008: 1032). Celebrations involving feasting with the dead in modern All Saints or Feast of the Dead festivals in the Andes, which occur around planting time and the start of the rains, are believed to lead to increased fertility in crops and herds (Bastien 1995: 368-369; Carmichael 1994: 83; Sillar 1992: 117). In the highlands, *machu*, spirits of the deceased who reside in pre-Hispanic funerary structures, are believed to cultivate potato fields at night (Sillar 1992: 118). In pre-Hispanic times and during the early Colonial period, the mummies of ancestors were considered to ensure fertility (Salomon 1991: 20), and the placement of tombs of *mallkis* in fields links ancestors to agricultural production (Sillar 1992: 115). *Yllapa* ("thunder and lightning") is a term used to refer to the Inca deceased, and may relate to the role of mummies in mediation with natural forces and rain bringing (Classen 1993: 92). According to the chronicler Cobo (1988: 125), the body of Inca Roca was paraded through fields in order to bring rain. The association of Inca royal mummies to rainfall suggests that they played a crucial role in agricultural productivity.

In addition to agricultural fertility, Inca mummies were associated with human fertility (Dean 2006a: 107). According to Cobo:

> ...they took great care to worship the dead bodies of the lords, especially their own ancestors, whom they saw as the cause of their birth. Everyone else worshiped these lords in order to please the Incas. To this was added the opinion (and it is the second reason why they worshiped them) that by preserving and respecting these bodies their progeny would multiply (1990: 42).

In contrast to the Western tradition, which tends to equate aging with diminished sexual potency and generally considers death antithetical to fertility, Andean ancestors were part of a continuum of fertility and had a sustained role in human reproduction, beyond the procreative act of producing offspring while living. In a sense, the number of progeny of subsequent generations may have been considered a reflection of an ancestor's sexual potency, and perhaps as the number of offspring increased, so too did the ancestor's perceived potency. In this regard, images that depict Wrinkle Face engaged in sex are entirely in accord with his identity as a *mallki*, because sexuality and ancestorhood are intertwined concepts.

The Moche association with deceased ancestors and sexuality may be vividly illustrated in ceramic vessels that portray living females grasping the fleshy phalli of otherwise skeletal beings (figure 4.14) or solitary skeletons that appear to masturbate. In these images, Moche ancestors may be seen to retain their sexual potency after the body dies and decays. Vessels bearing such imagery seem appropriate as grave goods for Moche ancestors, given their probable association with agricultural fertility and human reproduction. Benson (2012: 128) notes that vessels that portray a living female with a skeletal companion may evoke the condition in which they were interred, as high-status male Moche tombs often contain the remains of female attendants.[30] In the art of the Recuay, the highland neighbors of the southern Moche, sculptures that likely represent mortuary bundles (see DeLeonardis and Lau 2004: 89) portray seated, cross-legged figures with prominently displayed genitals, possibly alluding to the reproductive capacity of ancestors (figure 4.15a). While the sculptures may have been intended to be covered with textiles like Chancay "cuchimilco" figures and Inca Capac Hucha figurines, carved lintels, which spanned the entrances of Recuay mortuary structures, portray low-relief nude figures with arms and legs spread, drawing the viewer's attention to the genitalia, which could not have been covered (figure 4.15b).

Trees are linked to the deceased through Moche funerary practices and those of other Andean cultures. Moche burials are often marked with vertical cane or *algarrobo* posts (Benson 1972: 129; Bourget and Millaire 2000: 55-56, see fig. 48; Donnan 1995: 142), and wooden planks were frequently laid across elite tombs. In other instances, high-status burials were encased in cane frames, cane tubes, cane coffins, and plank coffins (Alva and Donnan 1993: 57; Donnan 1995: 125-135), a deviation from the simple cotton-shroud wrappings typical of lower-status burials. Other coastal cultures, contemporary with the Moche, used similar burial practices, which may suggest

---

[30] Zuidema (1989: 126, cited in Sillar 1992: 113) notes a colonial account that describes the tomb of a cacique under Inca rule named Caque Poma, whose tomb contained his mummy, flanked on either side by his ancestors and descendants. This arrangement recalls Moche vessels that portray an ithyphallic skeletal being that is surrounded by women and/or other skeletons.

Figure 5.14. Stirrup-spout vessel representing woman and skeletal being. Museo Larco, Lima. ML004341.

a

b

Figure 5.15. Recuay sculptures: a) Seated male figure. Museo Regional de Ancash, Huaraz, Peru; b) Lintel depicting felines and male figure. Museo Regional de Ancash, Huaraz, Peru.

that they viewed certain of the deceased as *mallkis*. *Huarango* logs laid side-by-side on top of high-status Nasca tombs and cane bundles on lower-status tombs, in addition to the presence of pacae fruit seeds interred with burials or individual heads, may relate ancestors to fruit trees (DeLeonardis and Lau 2004: 107). Silverman (1993: 174-194) suggests that regularly-spaced upright *huarango* posts in the Room of Posts at the Nasca site Cahuachi, which likely housed important burials, could have been related to important ancestors. DeLeonardis and Lau (2004: 110) liken the arrangement to an enclosed orchard. A Nasca burial of a decapitated male at the site of La Tiza contained a jar that served as a "surrogate head," and was decorated as a human head with a tree growing from it (figure 4.16; Conlee 2007: 441-443). The jar appears to affirm that the Nasca associated trees with certain deceased individuals. In some instances, the Lima culture, located in coastal valleys that separate the Moche and Nasca regions, interred wooden logs as simulated burials, which suggests the practice of *mallki* veneration (DeLeonardis and Lau 2004: 113) and probable material metonymical substitution of ancestors' bodies with wood.

Figure 5.16. Nasca "surrogate head" jar from La Tiza. After Conlee 2007: fig. 5.

The use of the wood of fruit trees for funerary markers and house posts suggests that the Larco Jar and other related scenes depict Wrinkle Face in his role as a *mallki* and ancestral progenitor. At the Moche site of Dos Cabezas, Tomb A was covered by three intact Y-shaped posts, similar in form to depictions of house posts on Moche vessels (Donnan 2007: 25, figs. 2.2, 2.3, & 2.9), including

the beam that sprouts from Wrinkle Face's lower back on the Larco Jar. Similar Y-shaped *huarango* posts (*horcones*), some with anthropomorphic faces carved on them (figure 4.17), appear frequently on the South Coast in Early Intermediate to Late Intermediate period contexts (Beresford-Jones 2011: 111-114, fig. 6.2), suggesting that in some instances, grave markers and house posts may have also been associated with venerated ancestors. The focus of veneration at the pan-Andean oracular site of Pachacamac, on the Central Coast, was a relatively unassuming carved wooden post that also may have been considered an important ancestor.

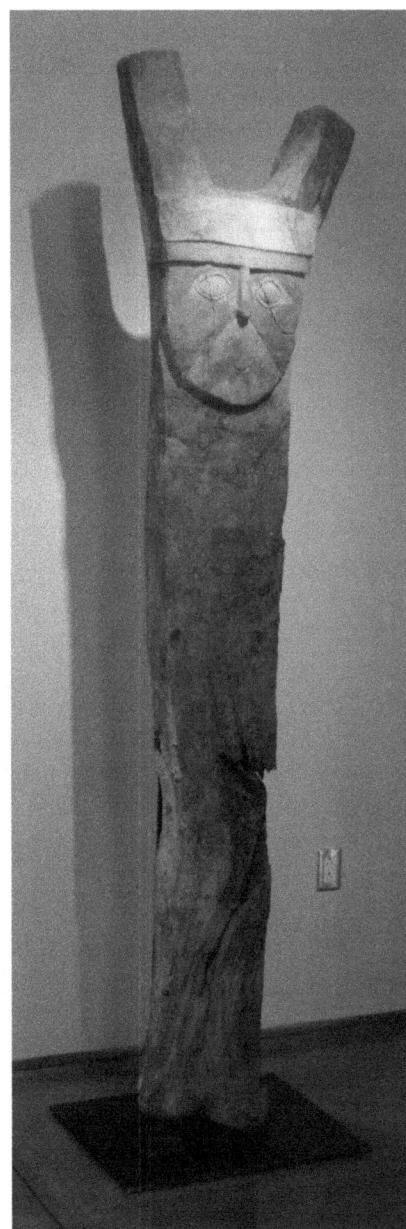

Figure 5.17. Ica wooden funerary marker, AD 900-1200. Private collection. Photograph by Britton Purser.

Evidence suggests that the Moche house, as a structure, was associated with ancestry and lineage. While most Moche burials occurred in cemeteries, some were placed under house floors (Donnan 1995: 153), an act of making place that unites the corporeal remains of an ancestor with the structure itself. Among the Recuay, who shared a number of cultural traits with the Moche (Benson 2012: 19), women are buried beneath floors and are frequently portrayed on top of roofs or in doorways of ceramic architectural models, suggesting that the house could represent the concept of a lineage or matrilineal descent group (Gero 2001: 42-43). In the modern Aymara village of Qaqachaka, Bolivia, house corners (called the hispanicized *turunku* - "tree trunks") are associated with the ancestral line, and ancestors are evoked through songs, libations, and drink during construction, which is completed around the Feast of the Dead (Arnold 1991). Quite probably, the fertilizing guano/*chicha* that the bird pours on Wrinkle Face's back during the act of copulation can be considered a foundational libation for the house post that renders the sex act fertile and causes the house beam, which recalls notions of lineage, to grow from the union.[31]

Based on several lines of evidence, it appears that Benson's hypothesis that scenes in which Wrinkle Face copulates with a woman (such as the scene on the Larco Jar) represent a mythic origin of the Moche is accurate. Whether this was only the case at Huacas de Moche or it was a widespread belief throughout the Moche region warrants further investigation. Wrinkle Face's relation to mountains links him to the widespread practice of the veneration of sacred mountains that are associated with ancestors. The juxtaposition of a mountain deity coupled with a coastal woman establishes the cosmological dualistic and complementary relationships between mountains and coast and man and woman, and the fertilizing exchange of fluids between them that perpetuates life. Wrinkle Face's plantlike features on certain vessels are consistent with Andean beliefs concerning *mallkis*, and his wrinkled face and characteristics borrowed from earlier artistic traditions suggest old age or antiquity. The house post emerging from his back

draws upon concepts of lineage inherent in Andean domestic architecture. The Larco Jar's imagery suggests that Wrinkle Face was promoted as an apical ancestor of coastal peoples.

As previously noted, Wrinkle Face possesses several traits drawn from Early Horizon Chavín and Cupisnique traditions. The fanged, grimacing mouth, on the otherwise anthropomorphic deity, links him to earlier art styles. Although kennings, metaphorical substitutions or transformations of certain visual elements, are frequently employed in Early Horizon religious artwork, they are not common in Moche art, but appear in Wrinkle Face's serpent belt and earrings. Rowe (1971: 102-112) noted several examples of archaism in Moche vessels in which Chavín forms were emulated, but were likely incorporated to evoke a sense of antiquity rather than to directly convey Chavín meaning. In response to Rowe, Cordy-Collins (1992) argued that certain Moche themes captured Cupisnique meaning despite differences in form and, rather than discontinuity, represented a continuous tradition. Wrinkle Face's features recall Chavín mountain deities in both form and meaning. The referents rely on a basic understanding of Chavín religion in order to register with the viewer and signify that Wrinkle Face is an ancient deity. A more useful approach may be to consider Wrinkle Face's Chavín characteristics as part of an invented tradition, a deliberate appropriation of antiquated motifs to suit the ideological aim of recalling an older tradition, and implying continuity that does not necessarily assume a misunderstanding or conceptual rift between form and meaning (Hobsbawm 1983). In representing Wrinkle Face as a Chavín deity, the Moche aimed to evoke the prestige of earlier traditions and suggest a greater continuity with the past, while casting Wrinkle Face as an ancient and ancestral being.

Ancestor veneration was a probable basis of religious practice on the North Coast during the Early Intermediate period, as was the case at other points in Andean history. Through ancestor veneration, kin descent groups trace their lineage through specific progenitors that are believed to maintain powers that can influence their living progeny. Ancestors may hold sway over matters such as health, economy, and warfare, and may be consulted as a source of wisdom (DeLeonardis and Lau 2004: 78). The veneration of ancestors is generally a conservative institution which reinforces filial obligation and the authority of elders (Calhoun 1980). Prior to the arrival of the Spanish, Inca royal mummies were revered as ancestors and kept in

---

[31] In the Huarochirí Manuscript (1991: 58-59), Huayta Curi, a son of the deity Paria Caca, competes against his brother-in-law to build a house. Huayta Curi lays the foundation and then relaxes with his wife, while later that night, birds, snakes, and other animals finish the house. The "relaxation" in this instance probably refers to sexual intercourse and the metaphorical initiation of a lineage. The birds, Iguana, and the dog in Wrinkle Face's copulation scenes appear to serve a similar role, aiding Wrinkle Face's consummation and the construction of the house-cum-lineage.

special chambers, given food and drink, consulted for important matters, and brought out on special occasions. *Mallkis* served as key focal points of genealogical reckoning (Salomon 1995: 339) and could function as "documents" that determined access to resources and political offices through inheritance.

Ancestor veneration is also an arena of social contestation among the living in which certain members benefit. As Salomon (1995: 325) observes, "death disrupts the durable interests vested in a system of power (especially rights in land and water or political office)." Through the evocation of revered ancestors, social actors are able to negotiate and justify entitlement to resources and rights to political succession (McAnany 1995). Likewise, descent groups (*panaca*s) in charge of the corporeal remains of deceased Inca rulers and their holdings could use royal mummies in the manipulation of power. Certain ancestor cults could gain prominence over others, with the benefit of gaining political clout and wealth in terms of offerings and services provided by adherents. On a general level, the establishment and maintenance of ancestor cults could have aggrandizing or factionalizing effects on the living as the perceived efficacy and authority of a given ancestor waxed or waned (Salomon 1995: 343-344).

There were several reasons why huaca centers such as Huacas de Moche may have promoted a paramount Moche ancestor. A number of factors such as variations in art style, architecture, and settlement patterns demonstrate that "Moche" was not a monolithic social entity or a unified expansionist state as previously believed, but was regionally and temporally diverse. As in other times and regions in the Andes, a basic principal of social organization on the North Coast during the Early Intermediate period was likely a system of kin-based units (Bawden 1996: 327-328), which is a system that is vulnerable to the splintering off of smaller groups at all levels (Quilter and Koons 2012: 137). The notion of an ancestor that superseded those of individual kin-based groups may have been considered beneficial and could have been promoted in attempt to foster regional stability while consolidating and maintaining power. The veneration of Wrinkle Face may have discouraged any one particular lineage group from attempting to claim absolute authority over resources by right of inheritance or direct access to the divine, while engendering a sense of unity among otherwise disparate groups. In Western traditions, the promotion of Adam as an apical

ancestor in Judaism, Christianity, and Islam, and the rhetoric of Christian spiritual kinship and ritual brotherhood supersede localized genealogies, claims of authority, and ethnic divisions that could otherwise prove damaging to the coherence of multiethnic religious movements. Similarly, huaca centers may have attempted to maintain control over ancestry by supplanting local genealogical and creation narratives among diverse groups of people living on the North Coast.

Although the Inca created an empire and were subject to different historical, political, and economic circumstances than the Moche, they nonetheless faced the same problems inherent in attempting to create a hegemonic discourse over origins and privileges of ancestry in a territory consisting of countless individual kin-based groups. Due in part to Andean methods of recounting history and varied constructions of historical realities among various classes and communities, numerous variations in Inca origin myths and histories survive (Patterson 1991: 43-45). One prominent tale involves the creation of the sun, moon and humans at Lake Titicaca by the deity Viracocha. After painting distinctive clothing on the people that he had fashioned out of clay and giving them different customs, food, and languages, Viracocha ordered them to descend underground and emerge from springs and caves at the places where they were to settle (Rowe 1946: 315). The Inca also claimed direct descent from the sun through the first ruler, Manco Capac, and in so doing, linked Inca ancestors to state-controlled fecundity (Sillar 1992: 111). The Inca thus attempted to claim a dominant creation narrative that accounted for regional diversity and supported the Inca royal line as the most direct conduit to the supernatural powers that controlled agricultural and human fertility.

As suggested by Quilter (2002: 179), huaca centers and rural elites shared power, likely through control of the flow of water. Huaca centers controlled water from symbolic locations, invoking the steady and consistent flow of mountain runoff through ritual. Elites living upstream could physically control the flow of water through force from strategic locations. Huaca centers such as Huacas de Moche claimed direct access to the divine sources responsible for agricultural fertility. The dynamic tension over power and the control of resources could be balanced by housing the remains of elites, either temporarily or permanently, at Huacas de Moche. Elite ancestors likely acted as mediators between their descendants and the cosmological forces and deities responsible for either agricultural abundance or disastrous drought or flooding. Huacas de Moche may have asserted Wrinkle Face as the paramount ancestor of the Moche, thereby serving as the focus of regional ancestor cults. Through this arrangement, elites could maintain or gain legitimacy through Huacas de Moche, while balancing power between sacred and secular concerns. Huaca centers could gain efficacy by housing the remains of important ancestors, and could benefit from offerings given by pilgrims in the form of goods and labor.

Art objects produced at Huacas de Moche, such as the Larco Jar, served as material manifestations of religious ideology. Wrinkle Face's exploits may have been based on stories of distant ancestors or common mythical narratives, but representing the myth in solid, material form lends validity to Moche claims and safeguards against revision, reappropriation, and misinterpretation. In other words, Moche artists may have attempted to solidify and claim authority over the meanings of stories and myths by rendering them in a clear, descriptive, and standardized visual style. Materialization of ideology serves the function of legitimating the objectives of dominant groups at the cost of others who lack the resources to produce materialized counter-narratives (DeMarrais, *et al.* 1996: 17). That the Larco Jar was made from a mold and shares its imagery with several other known examples suggests a concerted effort to regulate and propagate the narrative. While the question of whether or not Moche vessels decorated with elaborate scenes were strictly intended for burial with the deceased or served other functions among the living is unresolved, the impact of the message on the Larco Jar would have increased if it was circulated. The exchange of objects with Moche elites that were farther from core centers would have helped counteract potential political fragmentation (DeMarrais, *et al.* 1996: 23).

Depictions of Wrinkle Face are historically contingent, and the nature and frequency of his employment by artists change through time in the southern Moche region. Wrinkle Face begins to appear frequently in Phase III vessels (Donnan and McClelland 1999: 64), and depictions of Wrinkle Face and narrative scenes figure prominently in Phase IV (or the Huacas de Moche sub-style) and Phase V artwork. Scenes of Wrinkle Face battling sea creatures are widespread throughout the Moche region beginning in Phase III, but the Burial Theme, for example, appears to be limited to Phase V. It is likely that stories involving Wrinkle Face were emphasized, revised, or downplayed at different times and in different Moche sub-regions. The aforementioned vessel that was made in the same workshop or likely the same mold as the Larco Jar was recovered in a burial that dates to around AD 600 (Chapdelaine 2001: 80-81). The end of the sixth century was marked by environmental and social stress that led to the decline of Huacas de Moche (Bawden 1996: 264-269, 2001: 291; Bourget 2001: 96). An increase in fortified sites in the Late Moche period also suggests political instability (Dillehay 2001: 263). The appearance of Wrinkle Face copulation scenes as Huacas de Moche experienced turmoil may reflect a deliberate attempt to prevent further fragmentation through the circulation of imagery that suggests unified kinship, and Huacas de Moche ceramics may have emphasized narrative and visual clarity in order to appeal to a broader range of viewers and solidify the meaning. In other words, although Moche art is driven by metaphor, the highly representational style in relation to other Andean art styles may have served as a visual *lingua franca*. By underscoring common ancestry and broadly shared beliefs concerning agricultural fertility and the hydraulic cycle, Huacas de Moche may have tried to maintain its status despite a perceived loss of efficacy.

As Huacas de Moche fell into decline and Moche influence in the south diminished, Galindo, located farther upstream in the Moche Valley, rose in prominence. Galindo was likely independent of Huacas de Moche (Lockard 2008: 285), and may have formed in response to the troubles that plagued the larger site downstream (Bawden 1982: 287, 2001: 292-293). Several authors (e.g. Bawden 1996; Koons and Alex 2014; Shimada 1994) point to a major shift in ideology and the balance of power in the Moche region around AD 600 to 650 that may have been brought about by natural disasters, such as cataclysmic El Niño Southern Oscillation events. Bourget (1997, 1998, 2001) describes a graphic series of sacrifices, some of which apparently carried out during El Niño events, near the rocky outcrop in Plaza 3a of Huaca de la Luna, at the foot of Cerro Blanco. These sacrificial events, likely oriented toward Cerro Blanco, are reminiscent of Moche mountain sacrifice scenes on decorated pottery. After the sacrifices, the bodies of some 70 mutilated individuals were left exposed in the plaza to decay in the midst of torrential rains. These grisly findings indicate that Huacas de Moche was in a severe state of turmoil, likely brought about by flooding and famine, during times in which Moche IV pottery, including the probable double of the

Larco Jar that was found in association with the ceramics workshop, was produced.

Social organization and craft production differ between Huacas de Moche and Galindo. Unlike Huacas de Moche, Galindo housed palaces as well as workshops and temples (Bawden 2001: 289; Conklin 1990: 53), and was in a location that was ideal for exerting direct control over water (Bawden 1996: 286). *Cercaduras*, elite compounds at Galindo that appear to combine religious, administrative, residential, and funerary functions, more closely resemble the royal compounds (*ciudadelas*) at the Late Horizon Chimú capital Chan Chan, than any of the monumental constructions at Huacas de Moche (Bawden 1982: 302, 1996: 288-289, 2001: 294-295). Lockard (2008, 2009) has demonstrated that Moche V ceramics were produced at Galindo while Moche IV were still manufactured at Huacas de Moche. Although Moche V potters continued to represent narratives involving Wrinkle Face and Iguana in the northern Moche region, vessels in the highly pictorial Huacas de Moche sub-style are absent at Galindo, replaced instead with Moche V vessels that are generally decorated with abstracted designs that, while present, were not as prominent in the art of Huacas de Moche (Bawden 2001: 296). The rise of fortified sites during the latter part of the Early Intermediate period may represent a dramatic shift in the balance of power that had previously been negotiated and delicately maintained between coastal huaca centers and rural elites in the southern Moche region.

While the Larco Jar's narrative scene depicts a mythic sexual encounter between Wrinkle Face and a woman on the coast, themes of ancestry, regeneration, and agricultural fertility imbue the vessel with symbolic meaning and present a functional model for the workings of a vital cosmos into which human reproduction comes into play. In recasting Wrinkle Face, a Moche deity with traits that recall the Chavín tradition, as a progenitor of North Coast peoples and linking him to broadly shared Andean cosmological themes, Huacas de Moche may have attempted to supersede local genealogies and claim privileged access to the forces that make life on the coast possible. The Moche visual style would have been broadly legible and lent a sense of veracity to the scene depicted, yet symbolic meanings beyond immediate appearances would have been apparent to practitioners of Moche belief systems. The Larco Jar may represent efforts on behalf of coastal huaca centers to consolidate power and maintain stability among an increasingly fractious population.

Conclusions

A cursory glance at the low-relief panel of the Larco Jar reveals a scene that involves a host of anthropomorphized animals, and a deity copulating with a woman. Through analysis of the vessel within a broader conceptual framework of themes shared within the Andes, I have argued that the scene alludes to fundamental cosmological relationships between the mountains and the coast and male and female, a rich metaphorical language concerning fertilizing fluids and the hydraulic cycle, and a set of beliefs pertaining to ancestor veneration and the role of the deceased in relation to agricultural and human fertility. Resituating the vessel within its historical context suggests that its imagery may have been used as a means of solidifying the role of coastal huaca centers, and reinforcing social cohesion throughout communities that were prone to fragmentation.

In Chapter 2, I demonstrated that current views toward Moche art are shaped by modern attitudes and expectations concerning realism versus abstraction in visual systems, and spectacular archaeological discoveries of deceased individuals dressed as characters portrayed in Moche artwork have reinforced perceived differences in content and nature between the Moche art style and other ancient Andean styles. While there are key differences that distinguish the Moche visual system from other Andean art styles, particularly in regard to images portrayed on pottery, I suggested that a productive approach to the study of Moche iconography is to consider metaphor as a primary vehicle for conveying meaning. Subsequent chapters argued that several key metaphors concerning the body and the cosmos were shared by other Andean cultures. Although the style used by Huacas de Moche artists is visually descriptive and relatively naturalistic, Moche art should not be viewed as merely a record of historical social practices. While it is highly probable that individuals dressed as deities at huaca centers and reenacted myths depicted in vessel scenes, viewing objects such as the Larco Jar as a record of public events or a guide for performing ritual neglects the importance of myth as a point of departure for structuring ritual and reinforcing beliefs, practices, and behaviors by establishing a historical precedent or divine charter for the current or desired social order. It also does not adequately address the issues of why such images should be found on vessels

such as the Larco Jar, and why objects bearing such imagery should be placed in tombs alongside the deceased. Literalist interpretations of Moche art scarcely grasp the shared symbolism in art, myth, and ritual that conveyed meaning, structured thought, and determined how people should interact with each other, the world, the divine, and with objects. Scholars may ultimately gain a better understanding of Moche artwork by focusing on what is implied, suggested, or unseen, rather than on what is explicitly portrayed.

Since Moche artists made use of a symbolic visual language and did not aim to faithfully record historical events and practices as they were witnessed, scholars cannot rely purely on the imagery itself as a means of interpretation. Because we lack much of what could have been considered basic cultural and historical knowledge for adherents of Moche belief systems, two primary avenues of evidence for interpretation are open to investigators: archaeological finds at Moche sites and judicious comparison to the known beliefs and practices of other Andean cultures. It is apparent that Moche beliefs grew out of preexisting concepts and practices, and the strategic incorporation of prior traditions and views helped Moche ideology gain traction among potential followers. Undoubtedly, some Moche innovations were passed on to contemporaneous and subsequent cultures as well. Considering Moche art as a system that is built upon a substratum of widely shared beliefs in the Andes, but that deviates in its execution, is a useful approach for interpretation, although mindfulness of the historical and political circumstances specific to the culture, region, time period, and site is crucial for finding significant differences and understanding how the Moche made use of preexisting beliefs or discarded others to further their aims.

Although artwork produced at Huacas de Moche is rather unique in its naturalistic style and narrativity, like other Andean art styles, it incorporates symbolism as a primary vehicle for conveying meaning. While it is tempting for modern scholars to view Phase IV Moche art (or the Huacas de Moche sub-style) as the result of more sophisticated artistic and technical developments than in previous phases, leading to an increased capacity to portray complex subject matter (e.g. Donnan 1976: 62;

Donnan and McClelland 1999: 75), this view implicitly compares Moche artistic developments to the evolutionary model of technical artistic progression leading toward realism that has commonly been favored in studies of Western art beginning in the Renaissance. Such a view assumes that capturing realistic likeness is the inevitable aim of art across cultures and does not account for the sociopolitical reasons why using narrative and naturalism in artwork may have been more greatly favored during later Moche periods and not during previous phases or in other cultures in the Andes. Quilter (1997: 130) suggests that a shift in Moche artwork toward naturalism and narrativity may reflect changes in ideology. Analysis of the narrative scene on the Larco Jar supports an ideological shift and suggests that its imagery may reflect efforts to consolidate power by promoting a collective identity in the clearest possible visual language, and to reinforce the importance of the function of the huaca center. In this instance, narrativity and naturalism may have been the most effective means of conveying messages to a diverse network of rural elites.

In Chapter 3, I discussed Moche ceramic production, the workshop at Huacas de Moche, the social role of the potter, and the relationship between huaca centers and hinterland sites controlled by elites. That pottery production was among the most important means of conveying religious and ideological messages is affirmed by the central location of the ceramics workshop at Huacas de Moche. The lack of evidence of the production of domestic wares in the workshop also suggests that the vessels produced therein were not considered quotidian items, but were high-status objects that conveyed meaning consistent with the goals of the huaca center. Artists producing vessels and other objects in the workshops were economically, ideologically, and politically engrained in Moche society through the production and perpetuation of Moche symbolism (Rengifo Chunga and Rojas Vega 2008: 337), and may have belonged to an elite class (Uceda and Armas 1998: 108). The use of sophisticated mold-making techniques suggests that production was regulated, and in the case of low-relief scenes, consistency in imagery was a concern. The production of objects that materialize ideology serves the function of legitimating and maintaining elite control, and is linked to control over labor and the economy (DeMarrais, *et al.* 1996).

The conditions and methods of production of vessels such as the Larco Jar suggest that much of Moche imagery should be regarded as ideological in nature. As such, it is important to investigate areas of conflict or social contestation that individual art objects seek to address. The Moche region is no longer regarded as a centrally ruled empire or a single unified state, and we are only now beginning to recognize the internal diversity and potential instability of the Peru's North Coast during the Early Intermediate period. Located at the ends of river valleys, huaca centers were unable to physically control the flow of water from the mountains, and in this regard were at the mercy of rural lords living further upstream. The power of huaca centers may have derived in part from controlling the flow of water through ritual means and contact with divine forces at the *tinkuy* location where the river meets the sea. By housing their remains in temples, which were probably considered to be symbolic mountains, huaca centers may have allowed deceased elites to serve as mediators to mountain deities, thus ensuring against possible threats from rural lords. Through the mass production of pottery with the use of molds and in a broadly legible art style, Huacas de Moche may have attempted to increase the impact of its claims and minimize the force of counter-narratives through the circulation of goods bearing ideological imagery.

Chapter 4 provides an iconographic interpretation of the scene on the Larco Jar and other vessels decorated with similar imagery. I concur with other scholars who argue that Wrinkle Face was considered a mountain deity, and one of the paramount supernatural beings in the Moche religious pantheon. Wrinkle Face may have been analogous to Quechua conceptions of mountain spirits that are in charge of the flow of mountain streams and rivers, which are necessary for human survival in a region that receives little rainfall. I also argue that, as in known Andean belief systems, for the Moche, mountains were considered masculine entities and arable coastal valleys were feminine. The human body, as the fundamental basis for constructing metaphors, served as a model for understanding the world and its processes. The identity of the woman in the scene remains unknown, but the mythic sexual encounter between Wrinkle Face and the woman and its setting on the coast may symbolize the circulation of fructifying mountain waters to the ocean. The movement of bodily fluids during human reproduction is thus a microcosmic event that is echoed by the Andean hydraulic cycle. This pattern is also exemplified by the probable relationship between coastal huaca centers and distant mountains that provided water.

67

A cast of zoomorphic characters, including Iguana, a dog and anthropomorphized birds, populate Wrinkle Face's copulation scenes. While the precise nature of the relationship between Wrinkle Face and Iguana, and the dog that frequently accompanies the duo, is unclear, the birds are identifiable as maritime species that frequent guano islands. Numerous offerings found in guano deposits attest to the importance of these islands for the Moche, and guano may have been used as a crop fertilizer. In this regard, the guano birds underscore themes of fertility present in the scene. The most prominent bird in the scene, which may be a Moche guano deity, pours a concoction on the back of Wrinkle Face as he copulates with the woman. The concoction, which is likely *chicha*, is also metaphorically related to irrigation water, guano, and semen, which are fluids linked to fertility.

In Chapter 5, I pointed out that the house post in Wrinkle Face's copulation scenes actually emerges from his lower back (or sometimes his headdress), where the possible guano deity pours the concoction. The scene is therefore comparable to another pair of scenes in which a tree appears to grow from Wrinkle Face's back as he copulates. The tree and house post are likely analogous in Moche conceptions of materiality. The fruit from the tree, referred to as *ulluchu*, are collected by monkeys, which suggests that an additional set of scenes involving Wrinkle Face, Iguana, monkeys bearing bags containing the fruit, and a chimerical creature referred to as the Botanical Frog, are part of the same mythic cycle.

In the Andes, ancestors are often likened to fruit-bearing trees, as best exemplified by the Quechua term "mallki." I argue that certain characteristics displayed by Wrinkle Face, such as his wrinkled appearance and the tree or house post that sprouts from his back during coitus, demonstrate that he was considered an apical ancestor, similar in concept to a *mallki*. The reproductive capacity of ancestors continues well past the decline of sexual fertility and through death. The sexual event portrayed on the vessels probably represents the beginning of a lineage.

Moche religion may have been based in part on the veneration of deceased progenitors, and Huacas de Moche and possibly other sites may have claimed Wrinkle Face as a common ancestor for coastal peoples. Perhaps most importantly, fundamental beliefs about life, death, and regeneration and the organization of the cosmos may have been malleable and subject to manipulation in the service of sociopolitical goals. By employing metaphors pertaining to the human body and the larger cosmos in artwork, the Moche were effectively inserting and naturalizing their ideology into processes that would have been broadly understood by the intended viewers and they were claiming authority over the fertilizing movement of water from the mountains to the coast. Artwork was a potent means of conveying ideology, and perhaps the visually descriptive style employed by Huacas de Moche artists provided an added sense of veracity to the claims of huaca centers. The message portrayed on the Larco Jar may have been an attempt to consolidate power during particularly embattled times, as the power and perceived efficacy of Huacas de Moche waned and the site of Galindo, located farther upstream, rose to power.

To conclude, by investigating the ideological aims behind myth-based narratives, scholars can glimpse at the concerns, goals, motives, and meanings behind Moche art and its creators. For example, the Revolt of the Objects, which portrays animated weapons and animals engaged in a chaotic battle that ensued when the natural cosmological order was overturned, serves to reassert that the current order of the cosmos is the proper and most functional order (Quilter 1990: 61). On a basic level, the Presentation Theme (or Sacrifice Ceremony), which depicts the collection of sacrificial blood from captives that is presented to the Rayed Deity (or Warrior Priest), may set a divine charter for coercion and organized violence in the service of Moche religion, and the necessity of giving sacrificial offerings to deities. Copulation scenes involving Wrinkle Face likely aimed at instilling a broader sense of kinship among disparate groups through shared lineage and establishing the veneration of an apical ancestor as the basis for and means of ensuring agricultural and human fertility.

As Tilley observes, "things create people as much as people make them" (1999: 76). Objects are created in and for a specific social context, but they in turn act to reproduce and modify the social contexts in which people encounter and interact with them. The Larco Jar was produced as a luxurious object that conveyed specific ideological messages, and it served to reinforce Moche beliefs about social identity, mortality, and fertility to the individual viewer. It is unknown whether the jar's mass-production oriented method of manufacture would have increased or decreased its value in the esteem of the owner, but the vessel's probable placement in a tomb (like its double from Plaza 1 of

Huacas de Moche) suggests that it was a highly significant and valued object from the vantage point of those who buried it next to a deceased community member. Perhaps the placement of the jar in a tomb allowed a deceased ancestor-to-be access to a divine mythical progenitor, and anticipated the part they would play in mediating the forces of hydraulic circulation that assure the continuation of life on the coast.

Appendix 1

Timeline showing estimated timespans for the major pre-Hispanic cultural phenomena of the Central Andes by sub-region beginning with the Initial period

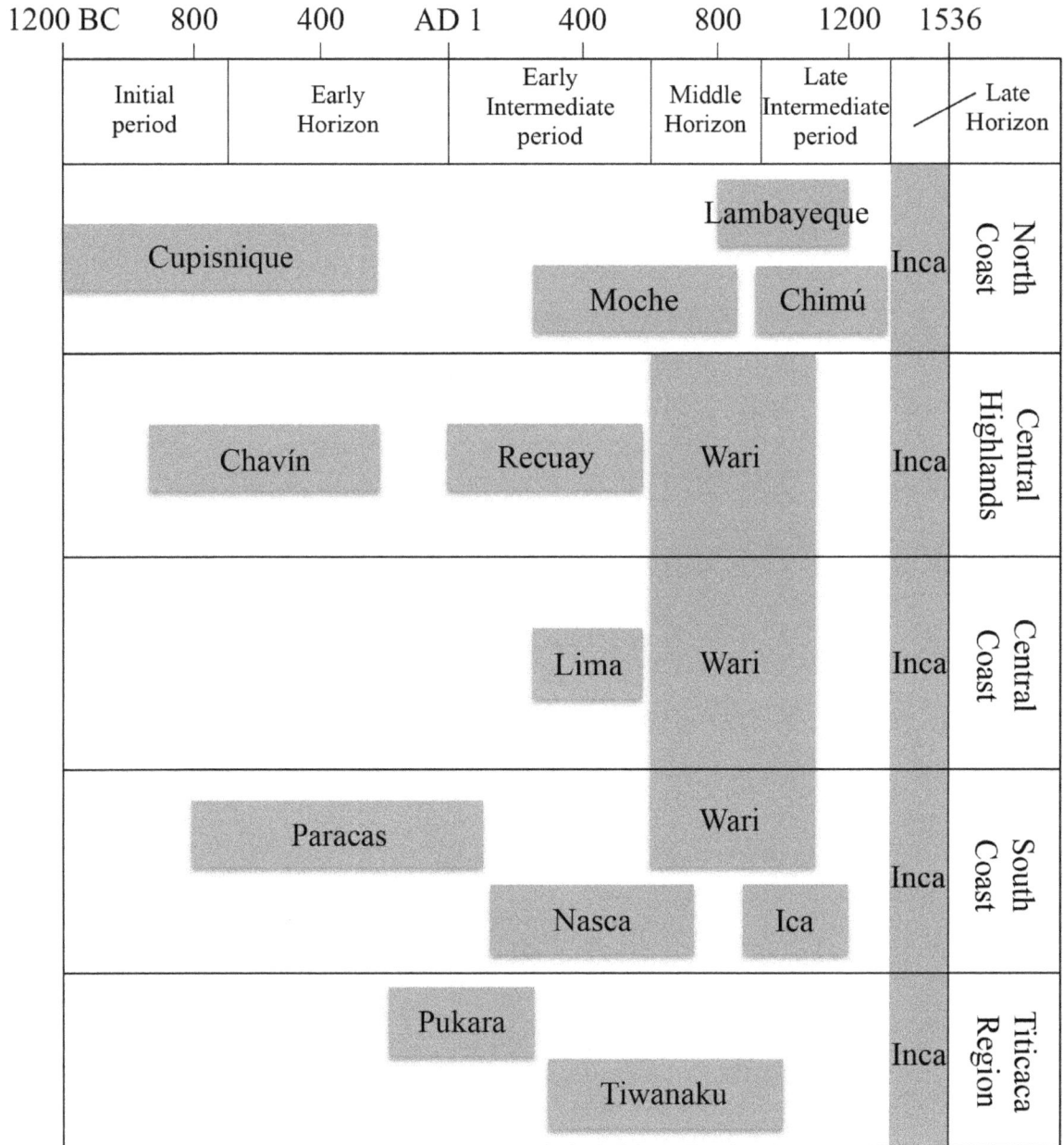

1200 BC	800	400	AD 1	400	800	1200	1536

Initial period	Early Horizon	Early Intermediate period	Middle Horizon	Late Intermediate period		Late Horizon

North Coast: Cupisnique, Lambayeque, Moche, Chimú, Inca

Central Highlands: Chavín, Recuay, Wari, Inca

Central Coast: Lima, Wari, Inca

South Coast: Paracas, Wari, Nasca, Ica, Inca

Titicaca Region: Pukara, Tiwanaku, Inca

70

Appendix 2

Timeline showing estimated timespans for the major occupations of a selection of Moche sites

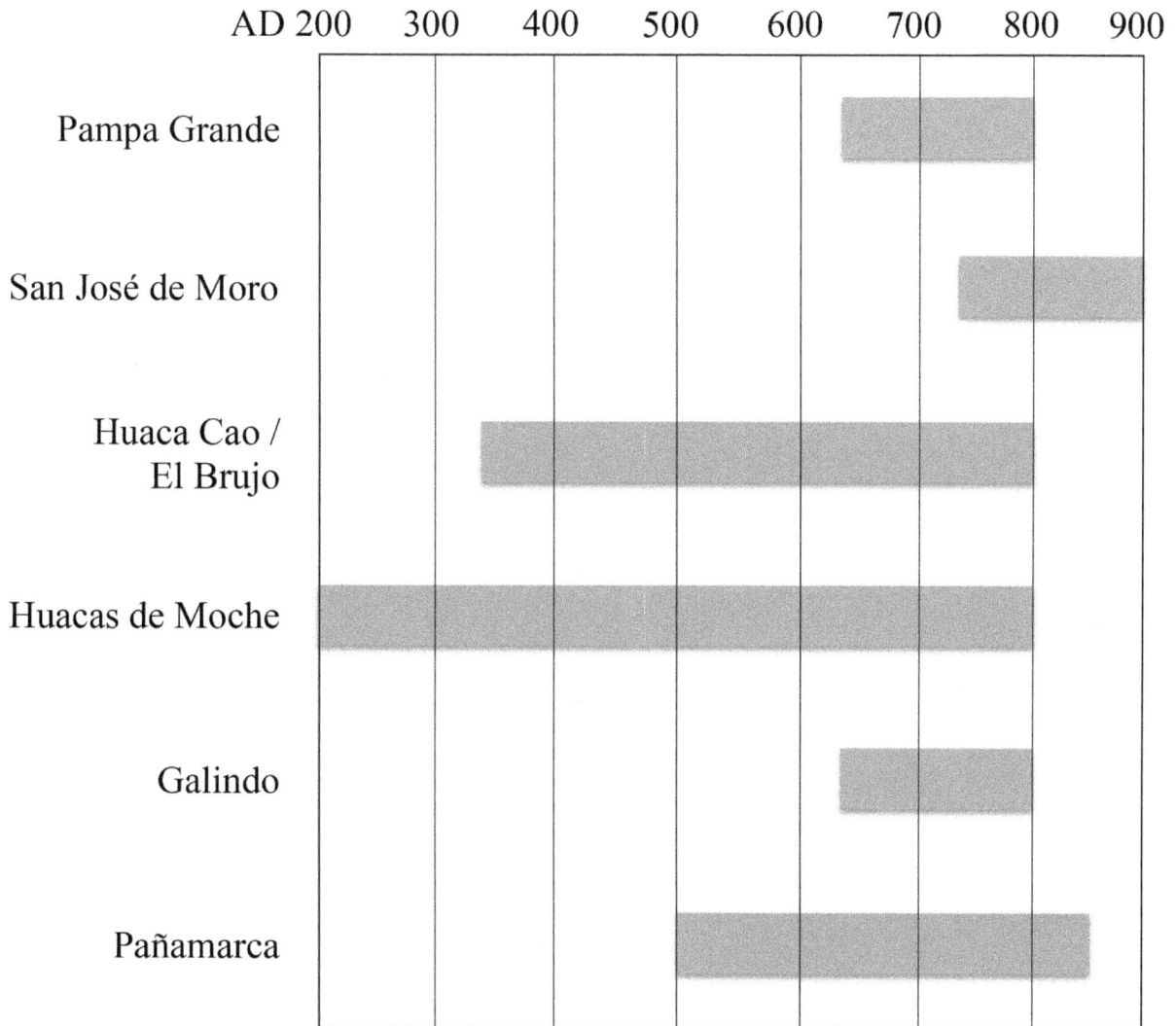

Appendix 3

List of Moche vessels portraying Wrinkle Face copulation scenes within structures

Specimen	Vessel type	Decoration	Iguana and dog	Birds and men	2nd house	Stirrup spout vessel	Body parts	Steps	Waves
Albert Fehling Museum*	Stirrup spout	Low relief w/ white slip highlights	yes	4 birds	yes	yes		yes	
British Museum**	?	?	yes	4 birds, 3 men	yes			yes	
Ganoza collection, Trujillo**	?	Fine-line	yes	4 birds	yes	yes		yes	yes
ML004360 Museo Larco	Spout and handle	Low relief w/ negative white slip	Dog only						
ML004365 (Larco Jar) Museo Larco	Neck jar	Low relief w/ negative white slip	yes	5 birds	yes	yes		yes	yes
ML004363 Museo Larco	Matrix	Low relief	yes	5 birds	yes	yes		yes	yes
Huaca de la Luna***	Neck jar	Low relief	yes	5 birds	yes	yes		yes	yes
Museo Nacional de Historia Natural, Santiago**	?	Low relief	yes	3 birds 2 men	yes	yes	yes (2 heads and 2 legs)	yes	
ML004361 Museo Larco	Spout and handle	Low relief	yes	5 birds	yes	yes		yes	yes
ML004358 Museo Larco	Spout and handle	Low relief w/ white slip highlights	yes	5 birds	yes	yes		yes	yes

*See Kauffmann-Doig 1979: plate XLI.
** See Donnan 1976: fig. 1.
*** See Chapdelaine 2001.

Glossary

Algarrobo – A tree of the genus *Prosopis* that bears edible fruit, and also known as *huarango* on the Peruvian South Coast.

Appliqué – A term used in ceramic production that denotes a mold-made or hand-built element that is attached to another ceramic object prior to firing.

Apu – A Quechua term for a sacred personified mountain.

Botanical Frog – A supernatural creature (also referred to as the Jaguar-Toad) that appears in Moche art as a frog or toad with jaguar traits and staple crops such as manioc and beans on its body. See figure 5.9.

Burial Theme – A series of painted scenes first described by Donnan and McClelland (1979) that appears in Moche V pottery involving Wrinkle Face, Iguana, vultures, a burial, and the presentation of conch shells to a seated deity. See also **Thematic Approach**.

Chicha – A fermented drink made from maize, also known as *aqha* in Quechua, which is frequently used during ceremonies in the Andes.

Chullpa – A Late Horizon above-ground funerary structure.

Collca – An above-ground granary or storehouse used by the Late Horizon Inca.

Depletion gilding – A process used by Moche artists that involves the production of an object in gold-copper alloy, which is repeatedly bathed in acids and burnished to remove the copper from the outer surface, leaving the appearance of pure gold. Depletion silvering is a similar process that produces objects in silver-copper alloy.

Espingo – A cleft seed that appears in Moche art, identifiable as a seed from the genus *Nectandra*, which may have hallucinogenic properties.

Fine-line – A Moche ceramic style generally consisting of finely painted imagery in red slip on a cream background.

Florero – A Moche ceramic flaring conical vessel with its largest diameter at the aperture.

Half fist gesture – A hand gesture that appears in Moche imagery, made by holding the fist aloft with the middle knuckle slightly elevated. It may have phallic connotations. See figure 4.16.

Hierarchical scale – An artistic device employed to indicate relative importance within a scene based on size, with larger size denoting greater importance.

Huaca – A Quechua term denoting a sacred location, object, or being, or as an adjective, referring the quality of sacrality.

Huaca center – A Moche ceremonial center with monumental architecture, including pyramidal structures, but generally lacking elaborate elite residential compounds.

Huarango – A tree of the genus *Prosopis* that bears edible fruit, and is also called *algarrobo* on the Peruvian North Coast.

Iguana – An anthropomorphic reptile that appears in Moche imagery wearing a vulture headdress and a sash. Iguana often accompanies Wrinkle Face in copulation scenes, the Burial Theme, and scenes in which they battle sea monsters. See figure 4.4.

Kenning – A term derived from Norse poetry used by Rowe (1967) to refer to metaphorical substitutions in Chavín-style art. For instance, snakelike hair may be portrayed as snakes. See figure 2.2.

Locator – An artistic device used in Moche art to indicate the physical setting of a scene, such as a dune to denote an arid environment. See figure 2.1.

Mallki – A Quechua term denoting a fruit-bearing tree or the body of an ancestor.

Matrix – A term used in ceramic production to describe the original handmade object from which a mold is made.

Muchic – A native language that was spoken on the North Coast of Peru at the time of Spanish contact.

Narrative Approach – A method for examining Moche iconography, devised by Quilter (1997), which interprets certain scenes that appear in Moche imagery as mythical in nature, and seeks to link individual scenes, or "themes," together into larger narratives. See also **Thematic Approach**.

Neck jar – A ceramic vessel with a globular body and a flaring neck. See figure 1.1.

Paccha – An Inca ceremonial object made of ceramic in the form of a digging stick, often with an ear of maize and an *urpu* attached to it.

Plectogenetic – A term pertaining to artwork in other media that is stylistically based on woven textile design.

Presentation Theme – A series of scenes in Moche art, first described by Donnan (1976, 1977), that portray the sacrifice of captives whose blood is collected in goblets and presented to a rayed being (known as the Rayed God or Warrior Priest) by an anthropomorphic owl (also referred to as the Owl Priest) and a female figure (referred to as the Goddess or the Priestess). See figure 2.4.

Qero – An Inca ceremonial wooden or golden drinking cup.

Quechua – A native language that is widely spoken in the Andean region, and was spoken by the Inca.

Revolt of the Objects – A series of scenes that appear in Moche art in which anthropomorphic and zoomorphic warriors battle against animated weapons and other objects. The scenes are relatable to widely recognized tales concerning a reversal of natural order in which objects and domesticated animals destroy humans in the mythical past.

Slip – A watery solution of colored clay used to decorate ceramic objects prior to firing.

Spout-and-handle vessel – A ceramic vessel type that appears in Moche IV and consists of a globular body and a curved tubular handle that connects to a straight tubular spout that emerges from the top of the body. See figure 4.8.

Stirrup-spout vessel – A ceramic vessel type common from the Early Horizon to Late Horizon on Peru's North Coast, which consists of a globular body from which two tubes emerge and join to form a single tubular spout. See figure 1.4.

Thematic Approach – A method for examining Moche iconography, devised by Donnan (1976, 1977), which seeks to identify individual episodes or characters that can stand in for the larger scenes, or "themes" in which they appear. Important themes in Moche art include the Presentation Theme and the Burial Theme. See also the **Narrative Approach**.

Tinkuy – A Quechua term denoting a ritually significant convergence of two opposed forces, such as two rivers or a pair of combatants.

Ulluchu – A comma-shaped fruit that appears commonly as an iconographic element in Moche imagery.

Urpu – A Quechua term for a large Inca vessel with a pointed base, a rounded body with handles on either side, a lug on the shoulder, a cylindrical neck, and a flaring mouth, which was used for storing and serving *chicha*. It is also known by the Spanish term *aríbalo*, based on the Greek *aryballos*.

Wamanis – Mountain deities and keepers of animals who are in charge of water, recognized in the Department of Ayacucho in Peru.

Wrinkle Face – A supernatural being that frequently appears in Moche art, generally with traits such as a wrinkled face, a feline headdress, a belt and ear ornaments terminating in serpent heads, round eyes, and fangs. He is occasionally refered to as Aipaec ("the Creator" in Muchic), Quismique ("Old One" in Muchic), God A, God F, the Fanged God, and the Serpent Belt God. Wrinkle Face is a central protagonist in a variety of painted scenes including copulation scenes, the Burial Theme, and battles against sea monsters, in which he usually appears with Iguana. See figure 4.2.

Bibliography

Alva, Walter

2001   The Royal Tombs of Sipán: Art and Power in Moche Society. In *Moche Art and Archaeology in Ancient Peru*, edited by J. Pillsbury, pp. 223-245. National Gallery of Art, Washington, D.C.

Alva, Walter and Christopher B. Donnan

1993   *Royal Tombs of Sipán*. Fowler Museum of Cultural History, University of California, Los Angeles.

Arboleda, Manuel C.

1981   Representaciones artísticas de actividades homoeróticas en la cerámica Moche. *Boletín de Lima* 16-18: 98-107.

Arnold, Denise

1991   The House of Earth-Bricks and Inka-Stones: Gender, Memory, and Cosmos in Qaqachaka. *Journal of Latin American Lore* 17: 3-69.

Bastien, Joseph W.

1995   The Mountain/Body Metaphor Expressed in a Kaatan Funeral. In *Tombs for the Living: Andean Mortuary Practices*, edited by T. D. Dillehay, pp. 355-378. Dumbarton Oaks Research Library and Collection, Washington, D.C.

Bawden, Garth

1982   Galindo: A Study in Cultural Transition During the Middle Horizon. In *Chan Chan: Andean Desert City*, edited by M. E. Moseley and K. C. Day, pp. 285-320. University of New Mexico Press, Albuquerque.

1996   *The Moche*. Blackwell Publishers, Oxford.

2001   The Symbols of Late Moche Social Transformation. In *Moche Art and Archaeology in Ancient Peru*, edited by J. Pillsbury, pp. 285-305. National Gallery of Art, Washington, D.C.

Benson, Elizabeth P.

1972   *The Mochica: A Culture of Peru*. Thames and Hudson Ltd, London.

1975   Death-Associated Figures on Mochica Pottery. In *Death and the Afterlife in Pre-Columbian America*, edited by E. P. Benson, pp. 105-144. Dumbarton Oaks Research Library and Collections, Washington, D.C.

1995   Art, Agriculture, Warfare, and the Guano Islands. In *Andean Art: Visual expression and its relation to Andean beliefs and values*, edited by P. Dransart, pp. 245-264. Worldwide Archaeology Series 13. Avebury, Aldershot, Great Britain.

1997a   Moche Art: Myth, History, and Rite. In *The Spirit of Ancient Peru: Treasures from the Museo Arqueológico Rafael Larco Herrera*, edited by K. Berrin, pp. 41-49. Thames and Hudson and Fine Arts Museum of San Francisco, New York.

1997b   Seabird. In *The Spirit of Ancient Peru: Treasures from the Museo Arqueológico Rafael Larco Herrera*, edited by K. Berrin, pp. 115. Thames and Hudson and Fine Arts Museum of San Francisco, New York.

2012   *The Worlds of the Moche on the North Coast of Peru*. University of Texas Press, Austin.

Beresford-Jones, David

2011   *The Lost Woodlands of Ancient Nasca: A Case-Study in Ecological and Cultural Collapse*. Oxford University Press Inc., New York.

Berezkin, Yuri E.

1980   An Identification of Anthropomorphic Mythological Personages in Moche Representations. *Ñawpa Pacha* 18: 1-26.

Bergh, Susan E.

1993   Death and Renewal in Moche Phallic-Spouted Vessels. *Res: Anthropology and Aesthetics* 23: 78-94.

Betanzos, Juan de

1996   *Narrative of the Incas*. Translated by R. Hamilton and D. Buchanan. University of Texas Press, Austin.

Bock, Edward K. de

2003   Templo de la escalera y ola y la hora del sacrificio humano. In *Moche: Hacia el final del milenio, Tomo I*, edited by S. Uceda and E. Mujica, pp. 307-324. Universidad Nacional de Trujillo and Pontificia Universidad Católica del Perú, Lima.

2005   *Human Sacrifices for Cosmic Order and Regeneration: Structure and Meaning in Moche Iconography, Peru, AD 100-800*. BAR International Series 1429. BAR Publishing, Oxford.

Bourget, Steve

1997   Las excavaciones en la Plaza 3A de la Huaca de la Luna. In *Investigaciones en la Huaca de la Luna 1995*, edited by S. Uceda Castillo, E. Mujica Barreda and R. Morales

Gamarra, pp. 51-59. Facultad de Ciencias Sociales, Universidad Nacional de La Libertad, Trujillo.

1998 Excavaciones en la Plaza 3A y en la Plataforma II de la Huaca de la Luna durante1996. In *Investigaciones en la Huaca de la Luna 1996*, edited by S. Uceda Castillo, E. Mujica Barreda and R. Morales Gamarra, pp. 43-64. Facultad de Ciencias Sociales, Universidad Nacional de La Libertad, Trujillo.

2001 Rituals of Sacrifice: Its Practice at Huaca de la Luna and Its Representation in Moche Iconography. In *Moche Art and Archaeology in Ancient Peru*, edited by J. Pillsbury, pp. 89-109. National Gallery of Art, Washington, D.C.

2006 *Sex, Death, and Sacrifice in Moche Religion and Visual Culture*. University of Texas Press, Austin.

Bourget, Steve and Jean-François Millaire
2000 Excavaciones en la Plaza 3a y Plataforma II de la Huaca de la Luna. In *Investigaciones en la Huaca de la Luna 1997*, edited by S. Uceda Castillo and R. Morales Gamarra, pp. 47-60. Facultad de Ciencias Sociales, Universidad de Trujillo, Trujillo.

Bray, Tamara L.
2000 Inca Iconography: The art of empire in the Andes. *Res: Anthropology and Aesthetics* 38: 168-178.

Burger, Richard L.
1992 *Chavin and the Origins of Andean Civilization*. Thames and Hudson Ltd, London.

Burger, Richard and Lucy Salazar-Burger
1991 The Second Season of Investigations at the Initial Period Center of Cardal, Peru. *Journal of Field Archaeology* 18 (3): 275-296.

Bussmann, Rainer W. and Douglas Sharon
2009 Naming a phantom: the quest to find the identity of *Ulluchu*, an unidentified ceremonial plant of the Moche culture in Northern Peru. *Journal of Ethnobiology and Ethnomedicine* 5 (8).

Cáceres Macedo, Justo
2000 *La Sexualidad en la Antigua Sociedad Moche Del Perú = Sexuality in the Ancient Moche Society of Peru*. Justo Cáceres Macedo, Lima.

Calhoun, Craig
1980 The Authority of Ancestors. *Man* 15: 304-319.

Carmichael, Patrick

1994 The Life from Death Continuum in Nasca Imagery. *Andean Past* 4: 81-90.

Carrión Cachot, Rebeca
1959 *La Religión en el Antiguo Perú (Norte y Centro de la Costa, Periodo Post-Clasico)*. Talleres Gráficos de Tipografía Peruana, Lima.

Castillo B., Luis Jaime and Jeffrey Quilter
2010 Many Moche Models: An Overview of Past and Current Theories and Research on Moche Political Organization. In *New Perspectives on Moche Political Organization*, edited by J. Quilter and L. J. Castillo B., pp. 1-16. Dumbarton Oaks Research Library and Collection, Washington, D.C.

Castillo, Luis Jaime
2001 The Last of the Mochicas: A View from the Jequetepeque Valley. In *Moche Art and Archaeology in Ancient Peru*, edited by J. Pillsbury, pp. 307-332. National Gallery of Art, Washington, D.C.

Chapdelaine, Claude
2001 The Growing Power of a Moche Urban Class. In *Moche Art and Archaeology in Ancient Peru*, edited by J. Pillsbury, pp. 69-87. National Gallery of Art and Yale University Press, Washington, D.C.

2011 Recent Advances in Moche Archaeology. *Journal of Archaeological Research* 19: 191-231.

Chinchilla Mazariegos, Oswaldo
2010 Of Birds and Insects: The Hummingbird Myth in Ancient Mesoamerica. *Ancient Mesoamerica* 21 (01): 45-61.

Cieza de León, Pedro de
1964 *The Travels of Pedro de Cieza de Leon, A.D. 1532-1550*. Translated by C. R. Markham. Burt Franklin, Publisher, New York.

Classen, Constance
1993 *Inca Cosmology and the Human Body*. The University of Utah Press, Salt Lake City.

Cobo, Bernabé
1988 *History of the Inca Empire: An account of the Indians' customs and their origin together with a treatise on Inca legends, history, and social institutions*. Translated by R. Hamilton. University of Texas Press, Austin.

1990 *Inca Religion and Customs*. Translated by R. Hamilton and J. H. Rowe. University of Texas Press, Austin.

Conklin, William J.
1990 Architecture of the Chimu: Memory, Function, and Image. In *The Northern Dynasties: Kingship and Statecraft in*

Chimor, edited by M. E. Moseley and A. Cordy-Collins, pp. 43-74. Dumbarton Oaks Research Library and Collection, Washington, D.C.

Conlee, Christina A.
2007   Decapitation and Rebirth: A Headless Burial from Nasca, Peru. *Current Anthropology* 48 (3): 438-445.

Cook, Anita G.
2004   Wari Art and Society. In *Andean Archaeology*, edited by H. Silverman, pp. 146-166. Blackwell Publishing Ltd, Malden, MA.

Cordy-Collins, Alana
1992   Archaism or Tradition? The Decapitation Theme in Cupisnique and Moche Iconography. *Latin American Antiquity* 3 (3): 206-220.

Costin, Cathy Lynne
2004   Craft Economies of Ancient Andean States. In *Archaeological Perspectives on Political Economies*, edited by G. M. Feinman, L. M. Nicholas and J. M. Skibo, pp. 189-223. University of Utah Press, Salt Lake City.

Cummins, Thomas B.F.
2004   Silver Threads and Golden Needles: The Inca, the Spanish, and the Sacred World of Humanity. In *The Colonial Andes: Tapestries and Silverwork. 1530-1830*, edited by E. Phipps, J. Hecht and C. Esteras Martín, pp. 2-15. Yale University Press, New Haven.

D'Harnoncourt, René
1954   Introduction. In *Ancient Arts of the Andes*, edited by W. C. Bennett, pp. 9-15. The Museum of Modern Art, New York.

Dean, Carolyn
2006a   Metonymy in Inca Art. In *Presence and Images: Essays on the 'presence' of the prototype within the image*, edited by R. Shepherd and R. Maniura, pp. 105-120. Ashgate, Aldersot, UK.
2006b   The Trouble with (the Term) Art. *Art Journal* 65 (2): 24-32.
2007   The Inka Married the Earth: Integrated Outcrops and the Making of Place. *Art Bulletin* LXXXIX (3): 502-518.

DeLeonardis, Lisa and George F. Lau
2004   Life, Death, and Ancestors. In *Andean Archaeology*, edited by H. Silverman, pp. 77-115. Blackwell Publishing Ltd, Malden, MA.

DeMarrais, Elizabeth Castillo, Luis Jaime Castillo and Timothy Earle

1996   Ideology, Materialization, and Power Strategies. *Current Anthropology* 37 (1): 15-31.

Dillehay, Tom D.
2001   Town and Country in Late Moche Times: A View from Two Northern Valleys. In *Moche Art and Archaeology in Ancient Peru*, edited by J. Pillsbury, pp. 259-283. National Gallery of Art, Washington, D.C.

Dobkin de Rios, Marlene
1977   Plant Hallucinogens and the Religion of the Mochica - an Ancient Peruvian People. *Economic Botany* 31 (2): 189-203.

Donnan, Christopher B.
1965   Moche Ceramic Technology. *Ñawpa Pacha* 3: 115-134.
1976   *Moche Art and Iconography*. UCLA Latin American Studies Volume 33. University of California, Los Angeles.
1977   The Thematic Approach to Moche Iconography. In *Pre-Columbian Art History: Selected Readings*, edited by A. Cordy-Collins and J. Stern, pp. 407-420. Peek Publications, Palo Alto.
1982   Dance in Moche Art. *Ñawpa Pacha* 20: 97-120.
1992   *Ceramics of Ancient Peru*. Fowler Museum of Cultural History, University of California, Los Angeles.
1995   Moche Funerary Practice. In *Tombs for the Living: Andean Mortuary Practices*, edited by T. D. Dillehay, pp. 111-159. Dumbarton Oaks Research Library and Collection, Washington, D.C.
1996   Moche. In *Andean Art at Dumbarton Oaks, Volume I*, edited by E. H. Boone, pp. 123-162.   Dumbarton Oaks Research Library and Collection, Washington, D.C.
2004   *Moche Portraits from Ancient Peru*. University of Texas Press, Austin.
2007   *Moche Tombs at Dos Cabezas*. Monograph 59. Cotsen Institute of Archaeology at UCLA, Los Angeles.
2011   Moche Substyles: Keys to Understanding Moche Political Organization. *Boletín del Museo Chileno de Arte Precolombino* 16 (1): 105-118.

Donnan, Christopher B. and Luis Jaime Castillo
1992   Finding the Tomb of a Moche Priestess. *Archaeology* 45 (6): 38-42.

Donnan, Christopher B. and Donna McClelland
1979   *The Burial Theme in Moche Iconography*. Studies in Pre-Columbian Art and Archaeology No. 23. Dumbarton Oaks, Washington D.C.

1999   *Moche Fineline Painting: Its Evolution and Its Artists*. UCLA Fowler Museum of Cultural History, Los Angeles.

Eubanks, Mary W.

1999   *Corn in Clay: Maize Paleoethnobotany in Pre-Columbian Art*. University Press of Florida, Gainesville.

Frame, Mary

1995   *Ancient Peruvian Mantles, 300 B.C. - A.D. 200*. Metropolitan Museum of Art, New York.

2001   Blood, Fertility, and Transformation: Interwoven Themes in the Paracas Necropolis Embroideries. In *Ritual Sacrifice in Ancient Peru*, edited by E. P. Benson and A. G. Cook, pp. 55-92. University of Texas Press, Austin.

Franco Jordán, Régulo

2012   El Apu Campana, la montaña sagrada moche. *Pueblo Continente* 23 (2): 292-307.

Gálvez Mora, César and Jesús Briceño Rosario

2001   The Moche in the Chicama Valley. In *Moche Art and Archaeology in Ancient Peru*, edited by J. Pillsbury, pp. 141-157. National Gallery of Art, Washington, D.C.

Garcilaso de la Vega, El Inca

1960   *Royal Commentaries of the Yncas*. Translated by C. R. Markham II. Burt Franklin, Publisher, New York.

Gebhard, Paul H.

1970   Sexual Motifs in Prehistoric Peruvian Ceramics. In *Studies in Erotic Art*, edited by T. Bowie and C. V. Christenson, pp. 109-169. Basic Books, Inc., Publishers, New York and London.

Gero, Joan M.

2001   Field Knots and Ceramic Beaus: Interpreting Gender in the Peruvian Early Intermediate Period. In *Gender in Pre-Hispanic America*, edited by C. F. Klein and J. Quilter, pp. 15-55. Dumbarton Oaks Research Library and Collection, Washington D.C.

2004   Sex Pots of Ancient Peru: Post-Gender Reflections. In *Combining the Past and the Present: Archaeological Perspectives on Society*, edited by T. Oestigaard, N. Anfinset and T. Saetersdal, pp. 3-22. BAR International Series 1210. BAR Publishing, Oxford.

Golte, Jürgen

2009   *Moche: Cosmología y sociedad*. IEP Instituto de Estudios Peruanos and Centro Bartolomé de las Casas, Lima and Cuzco.

Harrison, Regina

1989   *Signs, Songs, and Memory in the Andes: Translating Quechua Language and Culture*. University of Texas Press, Austin.

Hastorf, Christine A. and Sissel Johannessen

1991   Understanding Changing People/Plant Relationships in the Prehispanic Andes. In *Processual and Postprocessual Archaeologies: Multiple Ways of Knowing the Past*, edited by R. W. Preucel, pp. 140-155. Center for Archaeological Investigations, Occasional Paper No. 10. Southern Illinois University at Carbondale.

Hobsbawm, Eric

1983   Introduction: Inventing Traditions. In *The Invention of Tradition*, edited by E. J. Hobsbawm and T. O. Ranger, pp. 1-14. Cambridge University Press, New York.

Hocquenghem, Anne Marie

1989   *Iconografía Mochica*. Fondo Editorial de la Pontificia Universidad Católica del Perú, Lima.

Hocquenghem, Anne Marie and Jürgen Golte

1987   Seres Míticos y Mujeres: Interpretación de una Escena Moche. In *Pre-Columbian Collections in European Museums*, edited by A. M. Hocquenghem, P. Tamasi and C. Villain-Gandossi, pp. 278-298. Akadémiai Kiadó, Budapest.

Huarochirí Manuscript

1991   *The Huarochirí Manuscript: A Testament of Ancient and Colonial Andean Religion*. Translated by F. Salomon and G. L. Urioste. University of Texas Press, Austin.

Hultin, Eskil, S. Hendry Wassén and Wolmar Bondeson

1987   Papain in Moche blood ceremonies. *Journal of Ethnopharmacology* 19 (2): 227-228.

Isbell, Billie Jean

1978   *To Defend Ourselves: Ecology and Ritual in an Andean Village*. Latin American Monographs, No. 47. University of Texas Press, Austin.

Jackson, Margaret A.

2002   Proto-Writing in Moche Pottery at Cerro Mayal, Peru. In *Andean Archaeology II: Art, Landscape, and Society*, edited by W. H. Isbell and H. Silverman, pp. 107-136. Kluwer/Plenum, New York.

2008   *Moche Art and Visual Culture in Ancient Peru*. University of New Mexico Press, Albuquerque.

2011   Moche as Visual Notation: Semasiographic Elements in Moche Ceramic Imagery. In *Their Way of Writing: Scripts, Signs, and Pictographies in Pre-Columbian America*, edited by E. H. Boone and G. Urton, pp.

227-249. Dumbarton Oaks Research Library and Collection, Washington, D.C.

Jiménez Borja, Arturo
1985   Introducción a la Cultura Moche. In *Culturas Precolombinas: Moche*, pp. 17-51. Banco de Crédito del Perú, Lima.

Kauffmann-Doig, Federico
1979   *Sexual Behaviour in Ancient Peru.* Kompaktos, S.C.R.L., Lima.

Koons, Michele L. and Bridget A. Alex
2014   Revised Moche Chronology based on Bayesian Models of Reliable Radiocarbon Dates. *Radiocarbon* 56(3): 1039-1055.

Kubler, George
1962   *The Art and Architecture of Ancient America: The Mexican, Maya, and Andean Peoples.* Penguin Books Inc., Baltimore.
1985   Toward Absolute Time: Guano Archaeology. In *Studies in Ancient American and European Art: The Collected Essays of George Kubler*, edited by T. F. Reese, pp. 225-241. Yale University Press, New Haven and London.

Kutscher, Gerdt
1958   Ceremonial "Badminton" in the Ancient Culture of Moche (North Peru). In *Proceedings of the XXXII International Congress of Americanists*, pp. 422-432. Munks Gaard, Copenhagen.
1967   Iconographic Studies as an Aid in the Reconstruction of Early Chimu Civilization. In *Peruvian Archaeology: Selected Readings*, edited by J. H. Rowe and D. Menzel, pp. 115-124. Peek Publications, Palo Alto.

Larco Hoyle, Rafael
1939   *Los Mochicas, Tomo II.* Empresa Editorial "Rimac" S.A., Lima.
1946   A Culture Sequence for the North Coast of Perú. In *Bulletin 143, Handbook of South American Indians, Vol. 2*, pp. 149-175. Smithsonian Institution Bureau of American Ethnology, Government Printing Office, Washington, D.C.
1948   *Cronología Arqueologica del Norte del Perú.* Biblioteca del Museo de Arqueología "Rafael Larco Herrera". Sociedad Geográfica Americana, Editorial y Cultura, Buenos Aires.
1965   *Checan: Essay on Erotic Elements in Peruvian Art.* Nagel Publishers, Geneva.

Lau, George F.
2008   Ancestor Images in the Andes. In *The Handbook of South American Archaeology*, edited by H. Silverman and W. H. Isbell, pp. 1027-1045. Springer, New York.

Lechtman, Heather
1979   Issues in Andean Metallurgy. In *Pre-Columbian Metallurgy of South America*, edited by E. P. Benson, pp. 1-40. Dumbarton Oaks Research Library and Collection, Washington, D.C.
1996   Cloth and Metal: The Culture of Technology. In *Andean Art at Dumbarton Oaks, Volume I*, edited by E. H. Boone, pp. 33-43. Dumbarton Oaks Research Library and Collection, Washington, D.C.

Lockard, Gregory D.
2008   A New View of Galindo: Results of the Galindo Archaeological Project. In *Arqueología Mochica: Nuevos enfoques*, edited by L. J. Castillo Butters, H. Bernier, G. Lockard and J. Rucabado Yong, pp. 275-294. Fondo Editorial de la Pontificia Universidad Católica del Perú and Instituto Francés de Estudios Andinos, Lima.
2009   The Occupational History of Galindo, Moche Valley, Peru. *Latin American Antiquity* 20(2): 279-302.

Mathieu, Paul
2003   *Sex Pots: Eroticism in Ceramics.* Rutgers University Press, New Brunswick.

McAnany, Patricia A.
1995   *Living with the Ancestors: Kinship and Kingship in Ancient Maya Society.* University of Texas Press, Austin.

McClelland, Donna
1977   The Ulluchu: A Moche Symbolic Fruit. In *Pre-Columbian Art History: Selected Readings*, edited by A. Cordy-Collins and J. Stern, pp. 435-452. Peek Publications, Palo Alto.
2008   *Ulluchu:* An Elusive Fruit. In *The Art and Archaeology of the Moche: An Ancient Andean Society of the Peruvian North Coast*, edited by S. Bourget and K. L. Jones, pp. 43-65. University of Texas Press, Austin.
2011   The Moche Botanical Frog. *Arqueología Iberoamericana* 10: 30-42.

McClelland, Donna, Donald McClelland and Christopher B. Donnan
2007   *Moche Fineline Painting from San José de Moro.* The Cotsen Institute of Archaeology at UCLA, Los Angeles.

Moore, Jerry D.
1989   Pre-Hispanic Beer in Coastal Peru: Technology and Social Context of Prehistoric Production. *American Anthropologist* 91 (3): 682-695.

Mowat, Linda
1988   The Chimu Potter: Mass-Producer or Mastercraftsman? Some Thoughts Based on

the Spottiswoode Collection. *Newsletter (Museum Ethnographers Group)* 22: 1-33.

Mujica Barreda, Elías, Régulo Franco Jordán, César Gálvez Mora, Jeffrey Quilter, Antonio Murga Cruz, Carmen Gamarra de la Cruz, Víctor Hugo Ríos Cisneros, Segundo Lozada Alcalde, John Verano and Marco Aveggio Merello
2007   *El Brujo: Huaca Cao, Centro Ceremonial Moche en el Valle de Chicama/Huaca Cao, A Moche Ceremonial Center in the Chicama Valley.* Fundación Wiese, Lima.

Nash, Donna
2012   The Art of Feasting: Building an Empire with Food and Drink. In *Wari: Lords of the Ancient Andes*, edited by S. E. Bergh, pp. 82-101. Thames & Hudson Inc., New York.

Pasztory, Esther
1997   Andean Aesthetics. In *The Spirit of Ancient Peru: Treasures from the Museo Arqueológico Rafael Larco Herrera*, edited by K. Berrin, pp. 60-69. Thames and Hudson and Fine Arts Museum of San Francisco, New York.

Paternosto, César
1996   *The Stone and the Thread: Andean Roots of Abstract Art.* Translated by E. Allen. University of Texas Press, Austin.

Patterson, Thomas C.
1991   *The Inca Empire: The Formation and Disintegration of a Pre-Capitalist State.* Berg Publishers, Inc., New York and Oxford.

Quilter, Jeffrey
1990   The Moche Revolt of the Objects. *Latin American Antiquity* 1 (1): 42-65.
1997   The Narrative Approach to Moche Iconography. *Latin American Antiquity* 8 (2): 113-133.
2001   Moche Mimesis: Continuity and Change in Public Art in Early Peru. In *Moche Art and Archaeology in Ancient Peru*, edited by J. Pillsbury, pp. 21-45. National Gallery of Art, Washington, D.C.
2002   Moche Politics, Religion, and Warfare. *Journal of World Prehistory* 16 (2): 145-195.
2010   *The Moche of Ancient Peru: Media and Messages.* Peabody Museum Press, Harvard University, Cambridge.

Quilter, Jeffrey and Michele L. Koons
2012   The Fall of the Moche: A Critique of Claims for South America's First State. *Latin American Antiquity* 23 (2): 127-143.

Quilter, Jeffrey, Marc Zender, Karen Spalding, Régulo Franco Jordán, César Gálvez Mora and Juan Castañeda Murga
2010   Traces of a Lost Language and Number System Discovered on the North Coast of Peru. *American Anthropologist* 112 (3): 357-369.

Rengifo Chunga, Carlos and Carol Rojas Vega
2008   Talleres especializados en el conjunto arqueológico Huacas de Moche: El carácter de los especialistas y su producción. In *Arqueología Mochica: Nuevos enfoques*, edited by L. J. Castillo Butters, H. Bernier, G. Lockard and J. Rucabado Yong, pp. 325-339. Fondo Editorial de la Pontificia Universidad Católica del Perú and Instituto Francés de Estudios Andinos, Lima.

Rostworowski de Diez Canseco, María
1997   The Coastal Islands of Peru: Myths and Natural Resources. In *The Spirit of Ancient Peru: Treasures from the Museo Arqueológico Rafael Larco Herrera*, edited by K. Berrin, pp. 33-39. Thames and Hudson and Fine Arts Museum of San Francisco, New York.

Rowe, John Howland
1946   Inca Culture at the Time of the Spanish Conquest. In *Handbook of South American Indians*, edited by J. H. Steward, pp. 183-330. Vol. 2: *The Andean Civilizations.* United States Government Printing Office, Washington, D.C.
1967   Form and Meaning in Chavin Art. In *Peruvian Archaeology: Selected Readings*, edited by J. H. Rowe and D. Menzel, pp. 72-103. Peek Publications, Palo Alto.
1971   The Influence of Chavín Art on Later Styles. In *Dumbarton Oaks Conference on Chavín*, edited by E. P. Benson, pp. 101-124. Dumbarton Oaks Research Library and Collection, Washington, D.C.

Russell, Glenn S. and Margaret A. Jackson
2001   Political Economy and Patronage at Cerro Mayal, Peru. In *Moche Art and Archaeology in Ancient Peru*, edited by J. Pillsbury, pp. 159-175. National Gallery of Art, Washington, D.C.

Russell, Glenn S., Banks L. Leonard and Jesus Briceño
1998   The Cerro Mayal Workshop: Addressing Issues of Craft Specialization in Moche Society. In *Andean Ceramics: Technology, Organization, and Approaches*, edited by I. Shimada, pp. 63-89. MASCA Research Papers in Science and Archaeology, Supplement to Volume 15. University of Pennsylvania Museum of Archaeology and Anthropology, Philadelphia.

Salomon, Frank

1991   Introductory Essay: The Huarochirí Manuscript. In *The Huarochirí Manuscript: A Testament of Ancient and Colonial Andean Religion*, pp. 1-38. Translated by F. Salomon and G. L. Urioste. University of Texas Press, Austin.

1995   "The Beautiful Grandparents": Andean Ancestor Shrines and Mortuary Ritual as Seen Through Colonial Records. In *Tombs for the Living: Andean Mortuary Practices*, edited by T. D. Dillehay, pp. 315-353. Dumbarton Oaks Research Library and Collection, Washington, D.C.

Saussure, Ferdinand de
1983   Linguistic Value. In *The Course in General Linguistics*, edited by C. Bally, A. Sechehaye and A. Reidlinger, pp. 111-122. Translated by R. Harris. Open Court Publishing Company, Peru, IL.

Schaedel, Richard P.
1967   Mochica Murals at Pañamarca. In *Peruvian Archaeology: Selected Readings*, edited by J. H. Rowe and D. Menzel, pp. 104-114. Peek Publications, Palo Alto.

Sherbondy, Jeanette E.
1986   *Mallki: ancestros y cultivo de árboles en los Andes*. Ministerio de Agricultura, Instituto Nacional Forestal y de Fauna, Lima.

Shimada, Izumi
1994   *Pampa Grande and the Mochica Culture*. University of Texas Press, Austin.

Sillar, Bill
1992   The Social Life of the Andean Dead. *Archaeological Review from Cambridge* 11 (1): 107-123.

1996   The Dead and the Drying: Techniques for Transforming People and Things in the Andes. *Journal of Material Culture* 1: 259-289.

Silverman, Helaine
1993   *Cahuachi in the Ancient Nasca World*. University of Iowa Press, Iowa City.

Smith, Scott C.
2012   *Generative Landscapes: The Step Mountain Motif in Tiwanaku Iconography*. Ancient America 12. Boundary End Archaeology Research Center, Barnardsville, NC.

Stone-Miller, Rebecca
2002   *Seeing with New Eyes: Highlights of the Michael C. Carlos Museum Collection of Art of the Ancient Americas*. Michael C. Carlos Museum, Emory University, Atlanta.

Tello, Julio C.
1938   *Arte antiguo peruano*. Primera parte. Inca, Vol. II, Lima.

Tello, Ricardo, José Armas and Claude Chapdelaine

2003   Prácticas funerarias Moche en el complejo arqueológico Huacas del Sol y de la Luna. In *Moche: Hacia el final del milenio, Tomo I*, edited by S. Uceda and E. Mujica, pp. 151-187. Universidad Nacional de Trujillo and Pontificia Universidad Católica del Perú Lima, Lima.

Thompson, Donald E.
1963   A Mold Matrix from Peru. *American Antiquity* 28 (4): 545-547.

Tilley, Christopher
1999   *Metaphor and Material Culture*. Blackwell Publishers Ltd, Oxford.

Towle, Margaret A.
1961   *The Ethnobotany of Pre-Columbian Peru*. Wenner-Gren Foundation for Anthropological Research and Aldine Publishing Company, Chicago.

Trever, Lisa
2013   Excavating a Moche Epic at Pañamarca. Paper presented at the Andean Working Group, Cotsen Institute of Archaeology, Los Angeles, CA, October 23.

Trever, Lisa, Jorge Gamboa Velásquez, Ricardo Toribio Rodríguez and Flannery Surette
2013   A Moche Feathered Shield from the Painted Temples of Pañamarca, Peru. *Ñawpa Pacha* 33 (1): 103-118.

Uceda, Santiago
2000   El templo Mochica: rituales y ceremonias. In *Los Dioses del Antiguo Peru*, pp. 90-101. Banco de Crédito del Perú, Lima.

2001   Investigations at Huaca de la Luna, Moche Valley: An Example of Moche Religious Architecture. In *Moche Art and Archaeology in Ancient Peru*, edited by J. Pillsbury, pp. 47-67. National Gallery of Art, Washington, D.C.

Uceda, Santiago and José Armas
1998   An Urban Pottery Workshop at the Site of Moche, North Coast of Peru. In *Andean Ceramics: Technology, Organization, and Approaches*, edited by I. Shimada, pp. 91-110. MASCA Research Papers in Science and Archaeology, Supplement to Volume 15. University of Pennsylvania Museum of Archaeology and Anthropology, Philadelphia.

Urton, Gary
1981   *At the Crossroads of the Earth and the Sky: An Andean Cosmology*. University of Texas Press, Austin.

Vaughn, Kevin J.
2006   Craft Production, Exchange, and Political Power in the Pre-Incaic Andes. *Journal of Archaeological Research* 14:313-344.

Wassén, S. Henry

1976   Was *Espingo* (*Ispincu*) of Psychotropic and Intoxicating Importance for Shamans in Peru? In *The Realm of the Extra-Human: Agents and Audiences*, edited by A. Bharati, pp. 511-520. Mouton Publishers, The Hague/Paris.

Weismantel, Mary

2004   Moche Sex Pots: Reproduction and Temporality in Ancient South America. *American Anthropologist* 106 (3): 495-505.

Zighelboim, Ari

1995   Mountain Scenes of Human Sacrifice in Moche Iconography. *Journal of the Steward Anthropological Society* 23:153-188.

www.ingramcontent.com/pod-product-compliance
Lightning Source LLC
Chambersburg PA
CBHW061010030426
42334CB00033B/3437